THE PLAYS OF
GEORGE FITZMAURICE

REALISTIC PLAYS

THE PLAYS OF
GEORGE FITZMAURICE

REALISTIC PLAYS
WITH AN INTRODUCTION
BY HOWARD K. SLAUGHTER

THE DOLMEN PRESS

Published in the Republic of Ireland
by the Dolmen Press Limited
8 Herbert Place, Dublin 2

Printed by Hely Thom Limited Dublin

1970

Distributed outside Ireland, Canada and the United
States of America by Oxford University Press

Contents

We are indebted to AN CHOMHAIRLE EALAÍON (The Arts Council) for their assistance in making possible this edition of *The Plays of George Fitzmaurice*.

IN MEMORIAM

COLONEL WILFRED H. FITZMAURICE

1899-1969

Introduction

LIKE the folk plays, Fitzmaurice's realistic plays span the playwright's entire writing career. *The Toothache,* in fact, probably represents the author's first completed script, while *The Coming of Ewn Andzale* is his last play. Two of these six plays have never been published—*The Toothache* and *The Simple Hanrahans.* Three were published in *The Dublin Magazine*—*One Evening Gleam* (1949), *'Twixt the Giltinans and the Carmodys* (1943), and *The Coming of Ewn Andzale* (1954)—while the remaining play, *The Country Dressmaker,* was, of course, first published in *Five Plays* in 1914.

Had it not been for the single, very old typed script found with the effects of Fitzmaurice, *The Toothache* would have been lost. It was probably the first play Fitzmaurice thought good enough to save. Like many of his plays which followed, the 'scene is laid in North Kerry.' Fitzmaurice doesn't give the name of the village where the action takes place, but he does have his chief spokesman in the play James Hogan, the Gardener (or ploughman), give the following description of the locale:

> And, is it to view life you skelped down here to this capital village of our parish,—a little town with the population near a hundred, five public-houses and the Great House within the one fourth of a mile of it itself.

Hogan thus gives the nearest description found in any of the plays of Fitzmaurice's hometown, Duagh, and the 'Great House,' which is so very important to the action of *The Moonlighter,* becomes Duagh House, the Fitzmaurice ancestral home.

Some of the dialogue from *The Toothache* is as comical as any Fitzmaurice ever wrote, this speech by Jim, the Gardener, being quite typical:

> [*Estatically*] Didn't I know it would come with that drive and the black look that comes over you Mulcair and your tongue out. But it was a great holt you had of it and it a fine sound tooth itself. It's them stumps that do ever and always put you to the pin of your collar to make the right job of Mulcair, like the night you were at Michaeleen Quirke.

It is seldom that want of language troubled Fitzmaurice, but his language alone is not his only asset: his ability to create comic situations was, as this play testifies, with him from the first. While the extractions are performed without charge, Patsey soon learns that Mulcair is at his best for 'operating' when his cronies are there, not to hold the patient (for Mulcair sits on his chest) but to give their moral support. And they give their best support when the porter flows freely. Therefore, Patsey, to comply with custom, gives up a two-shilling piece for a gallon of porter which Mage, Mulcair's wife, goes for. The little farce, with its rich Kerry flavour and its robust humour, is indicative of the sixteen plays—written over half a century —that were to follow.

The Country Dressmaker has been George Fitzmaurice's only outstanding success in the theatre, and by even the most exacting standards it must be considered a remarkable 'first' play. An interesting newspaper review of the first production of the play, titled 'The Abbey Theatre—Cupid in Kerry,' written by a critic identifying himself only as 'AVIS', appeared in *The Leader* and provides several insights into the climate of the times and the audience reaction to the play:

> Since the memorable night on which Mr. Synge imparted, through the medium of the National Theatre Co., the result of his studies of life in the West of Ireland to a bewildered and ultimately horrified audience I have not found myself within the hallowed precincts of the Abbey . . . Time, however, dulls the sense of injury, and . . . I repaired last week to the Abbey Theatre, having warned my relatives to seek for me in the dungeons of College St. if I returned not at the usual hour, as they would no doubt there find me, expiating my offense against Liberty of Speech.
>
> The precaution proved unnecessary. The curtain eventually fell on a smiling author, bowing his thanks to an enthusiastic audience . . . It is to be regretted that now and again at the Abbey some play does not set before us some specimens of high-minded, noble-living Irish men of our own day, even if it were only to provide us with good examples which we might imitate.
>
> The plot is simple, yet for that reason the skill with which it is elaborated is all the more remarkable.
>
> . . .the staging was not elaborate, but its fidelity in detail was well in keeping with what one has been led to expect in this matter

on the Abbey 'boards', if so 'commercial' a word may be used in this connection.[1]

'AVIS' liked the play, even though he apparently regretted laughing at the foibles of his fellow countrymen. Joseph Holloway, after writing in his diary on opening night, October 3, that Yeats was a 'false prophet where Irish character is concerned' and that no troops were required to maintain order, went on to reveal that he was no more sophisticated than the critic of *The Leader*:

> Irish people can stand any amount of hard things being said of them if there is truth at the back of them, but what they won't stand for a moment is libellous falsehoods such as those contained in 'The Playboy' and such foreign-tainted stuff that makes them out sensual blackguards, cruel monsters, and irreligious brutes. Now the new dramatist, George Fitzmaurice (a young Kerryman, I believe) hits hard enough at times and his Clohesy family are anything but a lovable lot, nevertheless, their faults are human and Irish, and although it touches us on the raw to be confronted with such faults in public we wince and bear them knowing, alas, they are only too true in many cases.

It is pitiable that Holloway couldn't laugh uproariously at the Clohesys but found it occasionally necessary to 'wince,' for they provide much of the fun. However, it seems appropriate to recall that what the Abbey architect, the newspaper reviewer, and others may have endured was little in comparison to what other societies have endured from their best satirists. Today it is difficult to see very much biting satire in *The Country Dressmaker*, since the play is essentially humorous and the Clohesys and the matchmaker from the mountains, Luke Quilter, embody much of this humour.

Clear evidence that Fitzmaurice continued to improve in his craftsmanship as he grew older is found in the unknown revision he made to the ending of Act II of *The Country Dressmaker*, which must be considered somewhat weak. All previously published versions of the play reveal the following act ending:

[Exeunt MICHAEL, MARYANNE and ELLEN] BABE—It's some harm I did, I'm thinking, by what I told him. But how could I

[1] Volume I, *Abbey Theatre and Irish Plays*, compiled by the Abbey secretary, W. A. Henderson, now kept in the National Library.

help it all with the cute old withered sham of a Yank and the way he pretended to be enjoying it.
[Goes out]

In 1921 the play was reprinted in Dublin by George Roberts of Maunsel and Roberts, Ltd. (from the plates of *Five Plays*) and issued in green paper covers. When he died, Fitzmaurice had a copy of this edition in his possession which contains a number of minor alterations and additions, the most striking of which is the strengthening of the ending of the second act. He drew a line through Babe's final speech and wrote the following in ink:

> BABE—I have done harm codded by that old sham of a Yank. I'll do more harm or something will give. I'll break the chaney taypot; I'll break the chaney taypot. (handles teapot, reflects and replaces it on little table.) (Suddenly) I wo-ant; I wo-ant. (Bursts out door slamming it after her. As curtain falls noise of broken crockery is heard.)

Not only is the new ending more humorous and exciting, but additional interest in Babe and her clan is sustained. Babe's 'I'll do more harm . . .' strengthens both her mother's previous statement, 'He's not gone from us till he's married to her' as well as her father's last line of the act, 'If we could only get him once again into the clutches of the Clohesys.' The new ending achieves a better bridge to the final act, and we look forward to the final attempt by the Clohesys to get their man. This edition also embodies all the textual changes the playwright wished to make.

The principal feature of the plot that makes it so thoroughly realistic and understandable is that the matchmaking of the dressmaker to the Yank becomes a matter of clan supremacy and survival: The Driscolls of Knockanasieg (an actual Kerry family), the mother's family, are now weak, but are augmented by the Dillanes, represented by the Shea's neighbour, Matt. Opposing them is a larger and now more powerful clan, the Clohesys, who are liars, thieves, and landgrabbers (to mention but three of their minor vices) and who are led by their oldest brother, Michael. They learn that the Yank is bringing home that most sought-after commodity, cash, the very thing Michael needs to wipe out a heavy mortgage and Norry Shea, Julia's mother, needs to keep her from dying in a Kerry workhouse. The making of a fortunate match can mean the difference between business success or bankruptcy, life or death. It is readily understandable why the specialized craft of matchmaking should emerge in rural Ireland. Norry Driscoll made an unfortunate match with Peter Shea, and she strives to prevent her only child from making the same mistake. Michael Clohesy must swap one of his two daughters for the money with which to counteract the bad business deals which plague him.[2]

Not only were *The Country Dressmaker* and *The Playboy of the Western World* written at approximately the same time,[3] but they share the same essential theme, the contrast between reality and illusion, which theme is also central in much Irish dramatic literature of this century. Only in execution do Fitzmaurice and Synge differ. Both Julia Shea and Christy Mahon are sustained by belief in an illusion. Julia believes that Pats will return to her the way the fictional Sir Geoffrey returns to his Lady Gwendolen and makes her life happy ever afterward. This illusion must be burst in order for Julia to live with the truth that the Yank is a very ordinary man who loves her but who has lived in America not a saintly life but a life that might reasonably be expected of such a man in similar circumstances. On the other hand, because of the unexpected reaction from the motley Mayo group to his tale of parricide, Christy not only expands the illusion with each retelling of his tale but also is sustained by it. If his character were not developed through belief in an illusion, he would surely crumble when he sees his father alive and especially when Pegeen withdraws her love and support from him.

The late J. D. Riley sums up the assets of the play succinctly: 'A very subtle characterization accomplished through dialogue is the play's chief virtue.'[4] As good as the play is, the praise of Andrew E.

[2]It is interesting to note that W. G. Fay, the Abbey Theatre's 'General Manager and Stage Manager' at the time of the play's première, took the part of Luke Quilter, the matchmaker. J. M. Kerrigan was assigned the role of Pats Connor (The Yank), while Arthur Sinclair played Michael Clohesy.

[3]The first reference available to the composition of *The Country Dressmaker* is found in a letter written by Frank Fay to J. M. Synge in March, 1907, part of which is quoted in Green and Stephen's *J. M. Synge, 1871-1909*, p. 260.

[4]'Plays of George Fitzmaurice,' *The Dublin Magazine*, January-March, 1955, p. 7.

Malone seems too high: 'In many respects *The Country Dressmaker* is the most perfect comedy in the Irish Theatre.'[5]

Again J. D. Riley is, I believe, correct in calling *One Evening Gleam* 'a small and perfect masterpiece,'[6] for it is one of the most unusual and provocative of Fitzmaurice's seventeen plays. The play presents three very interesting women, each well past the prime of life. Two are widows, Mrs. Cleary and Mrs. Hannigan, who have lived a rather full life and who have no reason to hide their age; the other, Phoebe Tollemache, has reason to regret growing old, for she has never had a full life, must find vicarious satisfactions, and very much regrets never having had a husband.

There is much in the play to ponder, much about which one can only wonder. There is life, variable and elusive, and there is death, coming as it does in one evening gleam. Amid the complexities of life there is for a moment light and life, then death. Fitzmaurice tells us much about his characters, but much also is left to the imagination. The humour evolving from the interplay of these three very real ladies is rich; the poignancy of their story is moving. Once more the playwright reveals that he is a master of tragicomedy. Although Irish to the core, the play transcends the borders of a single nation. It speaks movingly of all mankind, continually struggling to comprehend a baffling existence.

At a time when the nations of the world were organizing a second world organization in the hope of increasing understanding between people and of preventing another world-wide holocaust, Fitzmaurice wrote his little tragicomedy. Although the playwright reveals a genuine sympathy for the characters in his play, nevertheless, he is still somewhat pessimistic of man's ability to understand and to live in charity with his neighbour. As an example of man's parochial vision, Nancy Hannigan tells Mrs. Cleary that the reason the old bachelor, who is a 'prodestant' and who lives in their tenement, doesn't take any notice of Phoebe, is that 'he's a woman-hater.' Nancy explains further, 'th' ould batchelor was jilted in his young days. He's a Corkman and they say they never forgive a thing like

[5]*The Irish Drama*, p. 171. It is all but impossible to ascertain what 'perfect' comedy is or should be; and it is, as well, a somewhat worthless speculation to rank plays.

[6]'The Plays of George Fitzmaurice,' *The Dublin Magazine*, January-March, 1955, p. 17.

that down in that part of the world.' Cork seemingly is as remote a place to Dubliners like Nancy as China. In *The Terrible Baisht,* John Daly, the family grocer, is referred to by the Kerry butcher, Shannessy, as 'a stranger to us from an outlandish place that's neither Limerick nor Kerry, and in its own county Cork is beyond the corn line, a woe-begone no man's land of a spot notwithstanding its being only ten miles or so away, is as foreign as Kamskatchka to the natives of this town. In *The Simple Hanrahans* this irony is employed still again. Daisy, the barmaid, thinks of the Hanrahans just as everyone else does: 'What harm but the simple Hanrahan's being almost furriners as I might say—why it's only three years since they bought the farm they have settled on here after coming from County Cork.' In *One Evening Gleam,* as in his other plays, Fitzmaurice is pessimistic of man's ability to break through barriers of miscomprehension with his fellow creatures.

'Twixt the Giltinans and the Carmodys was probably begun in 1919 and, therefore, represents Fitzmaurice's first playwriting attempt following his return to Ireland. Of the play J. D. Riley says, '... though it is amusing and extremely neat in form, the rather ghoulish under-tones leave the reader wondering. One suspects there is much more to it, but that little of it has met the eye.'[7] Maurice Kennedy saw even less in the play:

> It is an extension of the match-making tangles and stock figures of the returned Yank in *The Country Dressmaker,* but without the original touches which gave his first play its brilliance and humanity . . . Its cursory plot and slapstick characterization damned it to artistic failure, in spite of its occasional passages of delightful dialogue.[8]

Earlier Malone had written:

> '... [The] comedy ... did nothing to enhance George Fitzmaurice's reputation. It may be that in disgust at the treatment that had been given to his finer efforts he had decided to tickle the groundlings ...

[7]'Plays of George Fitzmaurice', *Dublin Magazine,* January-March, 1955, p. 14.
[8]'George Fitzmaurice: Sketch for a Portrait', *Irish Writing,* No. 15, p. 42.

But even in this tangle of familiarities there is keen characterization with no descent to the farcical.'[9]

Twixt the Giltinans and the Carmodys is Fitzmaurice's longest one-act play, but admittedly there are others that are of more lasting interest. The best thing about the play is the good craftsmanship with which it is contrived. Fitzmaurice uses a cottage kitchen with two exterior entrances and one interior entrance, and he needs each one to dispatch his eleven characters on and off with needed speed and dexterity. Considering the pace of the play and the climactic scene where matchmaker Clancy drives out all of the embroiled Giltinans and the Carmodys from the Daly cottage with a pitch-fork, it is difficult to see how Malone could say there was 'no descent to the farcical.' The play is a broad farcecomedy and was written as such; the plot clearly controls all else. Considering the pre-dominance of plot, it is a mark of good play-writing that the characters are as well differentiated as they are.

While one can agree with Maurice Kennedy that the plot is 'cursory,' the characterizations are more than just 'slapstick,' and there is no reason to agree that the play is an 'artistic failure.' Intended to be a farce or farce-comedy, it generally succeeds. That good farces in the theatre are rare attests, in part, to the difficulty in writing them. Fitzmaurice apparently set out to write a play he hoped would be accepted by the Abbey and would succeed with Dublin audiences. He evidently wanted to reestablish himself as a popular playwright. (To his credit is the fact that while waiting for the Abbey to produce this play he wrote his full-length fantasy, *The Enchanted Land*, which he probably considered a more original literary achievement but one which had less chance for theatrical success at that time.)

What Riley has written concerning the 'rather ghoulish overtones' of the play is interesting. Riley may have had in mind that Billeen's Aunt Shuwawn is sewing her shroud when we first see her, or perhaps he was thinking of the ending of the play when 'Old Jane' (really about the same age as the forty-year-old bachelor, Billeen) begrudgingly becomes a bride to fulfill her avarice. The final embrace between the two is characterized by the playwright as 'antagonistic' and 'grim.' This, indeed, is 'ghoulish' and a long stride away from

[9]*The Irish Drama* (London, Constable 1929), p. 172.

the more usual farcical clinch. It is as though Fitzmaurice himself were looking back over the contrived proceedings and mocking grimly his own creation.

Besides rather decided differences in plot development between this play and *The Country Dressmaker,* there is a marked difference in tone. Whereas the action of *The Country Dressmaker* is more serious and there is undoubtedly more sympathy for Julia Shea than for Billeen Twomey, the farcical plot development in *'Twixt the Giltinans and the Carmodys* brings with it a change in tone where the stature of man is more dimished and where he becomes more mechanistic and absurd. The Irish farce is, indeed, an excellent example of the kind of comedy Henri Bergson calls our attention to in one of his famous 'laws':

> The attitudes, gestures and movements of the human body are laughable in exact proportion as that body reminds us of a mere machine . . .[10]

Billeen Twomey's inability to decide either for Bridie Giltinan or for Madge Carmody dwarfs his stature as a human being, and Michael Clancy's forcing him into a marriage with Old Jane makes him appear even more like a robot than a man. And certainly Old Jane's precision in counting money and her avaristic approach to matrimony are, as well, somewhat machine-like. No other play that Fitzmaurice wrote is quite as pessimistic as *'Twixt the Giltinans and the Carmodys.*

Precisely when *The Simple Hanrahans* was written is difficult to determine, but use of such words as 'radio' disclose that it was written after 1925. As well, lines such as Lena's 'Good-bye, Pop' reveal that the language of the Kerry 'old folks' is not here being employed. Just as in *The Country Dressmaker,* Fitzmaurice sets no precise time for his comedy. In most of his plays Fitzmaurice follows the pattern of writing about life in the Irish countryside from the perspective of about two decades. Liam Miller recalls reading a draft of the play as early as 1948 and believes that it was begun even before this. From what Miller can recall Fitzmaurice wrote the play, hoping for an Abbey production. It is evidently the kind of play Fitzmaurice believed the Abbey wanted.

[10]Henri Bergson, from 'Laughter' [1900], tr. Cloudesly Brereton and Fred Rothwell (New York: Doubleday and Co., Inc., 1956), p. 79.

At times the farce-comedy comes very much alive, as it does in the first act when the prospective bridegroom, Pete Munnix, recalls the problem he once experienced in school of remembering the 'last spasm' of a 'pome,' and as it does in the final act when Pete and his bride, Lena, sing 'Sweetheart' with the same unfortunate lapse of memory happening to Pete. Although old Munnix and 'the mizzus' are little more than bland creatures, all of the Hanrahans, especially the cagey Michael, are real and comic, even though the device of having some of Michael's lines repeated by his brother, Morisheen, is used more effectively in *There are Tragedies and Tragedies*. Little is seen or known of Lena Hanrahan until after the bizarre second-act disclosure of her physical deformities, and had not this development been subtly foreshadowed in the previous scenes, the comedy would end all too abruptly. As it is, the audience comes to realize that Lena is both an interesting and an intelligent person and that her reconciliation with Pete and the ultimate victory of the Hanrahans falls right.

After writing *The Moonlighter* Fitzmaurice turned, as we have seen, to dark comedy, and primarily in the *genre* of tragicomedy he stayed for the remainder of his life. These comedies reveal that man is incapable of changing his environment. All of the comedies, whether folk plays, realistic, or fantasy show man as somewhat absurd in his pose. In the face of tragic events, Fitzmaurice must laugh. In an earlier play, *There are Tragedies and Tragedies,* he appears to say that this age is no age for tragedy, and in this play, in the words of Jaymary Gunn, here his *raisoneur,* Fitzmaurice underscores his basic attitude toward the world once more. Gunn, referring to the bride, Lena Hanrahan, says:

> Even if she bawled and screamed however pathetic it wouldn't be tragic, tragedy as the Greeks well know, having really a conventional mode of representation alien to our stratum in Society being applicable only to elevated characters such as kings and queens etc. it being denied to them the consolation of Bunyan's under dog, saint or humbug or whatever he was who perpetuated the bland generalization that he that was low need fear no fall.

According to Fitzmaurice man is too simple; his universe, too complex for him to cope with.

Begun, according to Riley, in 1950 and published in 1954, *The*

Coming of Ewn Andzale is the second of two plays Fitzmaurice set in Dublin. With *One Evening Gleam,* written five years before, Fitzmaurice clearly left the confines of south-western Ireland for the first time. Begun when he was about seventy-three, it is Fitzmaurice's last play.

The only criticism of the play I have found is in J. D. Riley's article:

> *The Coming of Ewn Andzale* is a mildly satirical comedy of Anglo-Irish Rathmines [sic, Monkstown]. It seems an amusing trifle . . . As Comedy, *Ewn Andzale* has little of the comedy and gaiety of Fitzmaurice's best work, and as serio-comedy it has only an indefinitive sort of suggestiveness. Some of the lines are very witty and one in particular is quite hair-raising, but the language on the whole is less interesting than in his folk plays.[11]

The dialogue throughout the play is, indeed, less interesting than that of other plays, and one of the reasons is that, while the lines may be read easily enough, they are insufficiently indicative of real speech. Too much ink and too little blood runs through the veins of the characters. One might suggest that Queenie, the older daughter in the family, get her head out of the text books and into the wind and rain, as Fitzmaurice must have done in order to hear, then to write lines in the folk plays such as Eugene's simple question, 'Yerra, how does I know?' or Peter Guerin's, 'The devil break your bones, what pinched you to skelp away at the glint of dawn?' An ignorant old peasant like Eugene's grandfather, Leum Donoghue, is dramatically more interesting than a schoolbook psychologist like Miss Davenport.

Ewn Andzale is not without humour, but its humour is rather scarce. The 'hair-raising' line Riley referred to belongs probably to Queenie, who explains her emphatic response to Bridget's scream and to her explanation that a mouse ran up her leg:

> Without any scientific knowledge of humanity or of anything else you are of course completely ignorant of the fact that there's a certain section of the female anatomy that is allergic to mice.

The reaction of the family to Queenie's explanation, especially that

[11]'Plays of George Fitzmaurice,' *Dublin Magazine,* January-March, 1955, p. 17.

of her mother, is one of shock, but, as a result, one likes Queenie a little more and one is less inclined to be irritated by her punctilious attack on her mother.

Ewn Andzale ends more happily than most Fitzmaurice plays. The arrival of Silas averts a show-down between Mrs. Davenport and Queenie, and there is little distinguishable difference between the mysterious 'Ewn Andzale,' Uncle Silas, or Father Christmas. The ending of the play is reminiscent of the ending of *Professor Tim*, George Shiel's most successful comedy, when the disclosure that Uncle Tim is actually wealthy and not a pauper too easily solves the financial difficulties of the young lovers and mars what had been before a strong conflict. The kind of 'happy ending' found in *The Country Dressmaker* or *The Enchanted Land* is more oblique and there is no sense of strict poetic justice, but the endings of these two plays are essentially more honest and more satisfying than the somewhat contrived ending of *The Coming of Ewn Andzale*.

Thus Fitzmaurice's six realistic plays reveal the playwright at the extremes of his ability. While *The County Dressmaker* and *One Evening Gleam* are among his finest achievements, *The Simple Hanrahans* and especially *The Coming of Ewn Andzale* are perhaps his weakest plays. *The Toothache* represents, in retrospect, a promising beginning to the long writing career the playwright enjoyed. In his strolls through Dublin, as well as in his hikes about North Kerry, Fitzmaurice viewed life quietly, rather objectively, too seldom, it seems, entering in. The life he observed evidently was harsh, often somber, sometimes filled with raucous laughter, for his predominately dark comedies reflect this kind of life, this kind of observer.

HOWARD K. SLAUGHTER

The Toothache

IN ONE ACT

First printed in THE MALAHAT REVIEW No. 1, Victoria, British Columbia, January, 1967.

CHARACTERS

MULCAIR, *the smith*
JIM, *the ploughman*
NEDDY, *the poet*
CONNY, *the weaver*
PATSEY DUNN
MAGE, *Mulcair's wife*

PLACE

Mulcair's Forge

The Toothache

The Scene takes place in the interior of village forge, north Kerry. At rise of curtain Mulcair, Jim, Neddy and Conny are seated in various positions, smoking. Enter Patsey Dunn. He has a bandage of red flannel tied about his head and face.

PATSEY   Good morning kindly, gentlemen. Patsey Dunn is my name, and it's from Meenscubawn I come.

JIM   [*rises, goes a step towards* PATSEY *and takes pipe out of his mouth*] Why, is it now?—From that wild place away in the mountains entirely?

PATSEY   It is so then, and [*proudly*] it is every step of the twelve miles I did in less than two hours and a quarter by the sun.

JIM   [*with affected wonderment*] Oh Mullowmay! And, is it to view life you skelped down here to this capital village of our parish,—a little town I may say with the population near a hundred, five public-houses and the Great House within the one fourth of a mile of it atself.

PATSEY   It is not then, sir, though it's a grand place entirely, for 'tis hardly able I am to open my eyes atself with a head as big as a pot on me from a belter of a toothache in these three teeth and you could hear the pain that's in them and they having every lep inside in my head.

JIM   [*sympathetically*] Ove! Ove!

PATSEY   It's over a fortnight the agony is working me, and 'tisn't the size of a wran it has left me in the heel, gentlemen, but the head being swelled by me.

JIM   [*very sympathetically*] Oh fodha, isn't that a fright!

PATSEY   It's recommendations I got to come to one Mulcair the smith.

JIM   [*earnestly*] And I am thinking it isn't far out of your way you are, and it's for your good that man was that put you on the track of Mulcair.

PATSEY   It's in the market town of Lyre I heard it atself, and I to ramble in there a yesterday thinking of having them teeth pulled by the apothecary; but in sure, wouldn't he charge me a shilling.

JIM   Big fool you'd be to be throwing money away on a rogue of an apothecary, and you a poor man's son I'd say by the cut of your clothes.

PATSEY   That's what Matteen Donohoe said to me and we to meet in the Square; 'twas him gave me the great recommendations to come to Mulcair the smith. Bear up with the toothache to-night, says he, and fire down to Mulcair in the morning and 'tisn't charging you he'll be like them rogues of apothecaries, says Matteen.

JIM   Houl! Is it in your senses you are and to be making mention of charges overright Mulcair the smith?

PATSEY   Sure, I wouldn't for the world your honour [*Jim frowns*] —Sir, I mean. 'Your honour' slipped from me for it's in the habit I am of saying it to a County Councillor above in Meenscubawn that I do be herding for,—for fear you might think it was codding you I was, sir.

JIM   [*doubtfully*] I see, faith. [*more freely*] It's a civil conversible man I am, but it's a good job for you it isn't to him [*pointing at* MULCAIR] you said it; it might take pains to persuade him it wasn't a hambug, and God help you! if it wasn't to believe you he did.

PATSEY   Is it the big black baist of a man in the corner, sir?

JIM   Houl! or it's in jelly you'll be entirely from that awkward gob in you from the mountains,—calling that ugly name on the bravest man in this barony, and in the barony of Traghticonnor along with it if I said it, and it's no surprise 'twould make for me if the match of him wasn't to be found in the baronies of Corkaguiny and Iveragh atself.

CONNY   [*bitterly*] What little dread there is in my clipper from Meencubawn and four of us here fornenst him.

NEDDY   Isn't it great work that pain and toothache atself can't put a stop to the ignorance and savagery bulging out of these mountainy people. [PATSEY *turns as if going to fly*]

JIM   [*catches him by arm*] You needn't be minding Neddy and Conny at all. It's my best I'll do for you to make spir-spar of it with him [*goes to* MULCAIR.] Big black baist of a man only slipped from him, and he a mountaineer. 'Tisn't too bad you'll be taking it entirely?

4

MULCAIR [*with a grunt*] Devil a hair I care.

JIM [*goes to* PATSEY] 'Tis all right now. Times you couldn't put him out of humour,—according to the way he'd be in or what stock he might take of what would be running in your mind. He's a fright if he's roused, but it's the easiest man in the world he is to deal with if you take him nicely.

PATSEY It's all humility I'll be your honour,—I mean sir, again.

JIM [*drily*] Ah! [*pleasantly as* PATSEY *shows terror*] That will do now; don't be apologizing any more.

PATSEY Is it here, you'll be pulling them teeth for me sir?

JIM [*laughing heartily*] Faith, 'tisn't I that will pull them, what would I be doing with pulling teeth, you little fooleen?

PATSEY Didn't I think you were the man of the house,—the man of the forge I mean.

JIM It must be I being a conversible man made that crack into your head. That's him [*pointing at* MULCAIR] Mulcair the smith; Mulcair the smith!

PATSEY [*nervously, to* MULCAIR] Oh, God bless your sir! God save you kindly!

JIM Ye! Don't be a bit in dread of him; it's the best friend you ever met in your life you see in Mulcair the smith. They calls me Jim the Gardener, but [*proudly*] James Hogan is my name. Whist you devil [*nudging* PATSEY] wasn't my mother one of the Sullivans of Banemore? [*speaking more loudly*] That's Conny the weaver and Neddy the Poet,—all friends of Mulcair and we drops in here regular. You couldn't come in a better time to have them teeth drawn. Mulcair don't ever be in the right blood for drawing till we're here; moreover Neddy the poet. It's teeth for the world Mulcair can pull out, when he has Neddy to sing for him one of them old ballads—one of Neddy's own makes wouldn't do Mulcair at all, but it's a fine voice Neddy has I am telling you, and it's wonderful soothing entirely the song do be to them having their teeth drawn. It's all good sort of people that's around you here; be pleasant and jolly in yourself the same as you'd be above at home.

PATSEY [*ecstatically*] It's in great heart and wind I am now entirely; it's something good must have pinched me surely to make a start the time I did; fasting atself; with cabbage boiling in the pot and the mother making tapes to keep me to eat of it.

JIM Pshough! cabbage. 'Tisn't cabbage you want the way you are with that toothache. A share of porter would put great life into you; but, I'll engage 'twasn't to pass up Miss Clancy's you wid without having some tint?

PATSEY 'Twas griping I was for it, but being shy and ashamed and I alone. It takes a brazen man to call for a drink by himself.

JIM [*sympathetically*] Gospel truth!—and 'tisn't any good you'd find in it if you did, atself.

CONNY [*sardonically*] Maybe he hadn't the heart even to buy a bottle for himself; mountainy misers always!

JIM [*to* PATSEY] Don't mind Conny—cranky in himself—no harm in him but that failing. I knew a man from the mountains—

NEDDY I knew a fine boozer of a woman from the mountains; Mary Car— [JIM *rushes to him*]

JIM Houl about that woman from Meenscubawn; weren't the Carmodys and Flynns related?

PATSEY Was it Mary Carmody he said?

JIM [*laughing*] Don't mind Neddy; he don't know what he do be saying when he goes ravelling about women and he scraping after them since he was the size of a sod of turf, like poets do be ever and always. It's got stuck in him he's acquainted with every female in the parish and has put the comether on half of them. They don't take no notice of him,—no harm in him but that talk. But I knew a great man from the mountains, one Michael Tobin. God rest him! he's dead now. No fear he wouldn't prove himself a man wherever he'd go;—no fear he'd let the second drink pass without calling for his share. The poor man! it's a tooth he had pulled here of a day by Mulcair and indeed 'twas spunky enough he sent out for his share of drink. They all sends out for some drop of porter now that are having their teeth pulled here; it's a custom now with them someway however it come to be, but indeed I don't know in the wide world what they want doing it for either.

PATSEY Wouldn't I send out for my share?

JIM You'll do no such thing and you a stranger and a poor boy.

PATSEY Why wouldn't I then? How much would do I wonder?

JIM It's a bad thing for a man to be too free in himself, but it's a drop badly you'd want yourself. A gallon would be plenty for the four of us.

6

PATSEY I have a two-shilling piece [*pulling it out of waistcoat pocket*]

JIM All right. It's Mulcair's wife goes for the porter. She generally brings cakes to the children if there's a few pence coming in the change,—no one bothers about a couple of coppers. [*goes to door*] Mage! [*pause. Comes back*] It's gone she is for it. Be roused and hearty in yourself now, and after having the sup, my hand to you, 'tisn't long till you'll be free of them teeth and shut of that pain entirely.

MULCAIR [*jumping up*] By jaymini it's in great blood I am now! Where's my pinshers? [*searches for it in corner*]

JIM Isn't Mulcair a great man; isn't he a wonderful man entirely?

PATSEY Isn't he great, great! Is it by the three of ye I am to be held sir?

JIM [*laughing*] Held! No need on you to be held here I am telling you.

PATSEY [*in great astonishment*] No need on me to be held with my three teeth being pulled!

JIM There's one of the great benefits in coming to Mulcair. No holding. No tooplaish. Quietness.

PATSEY That's the greatest wonder I ever seen not to be held.

JIM The old way is done away with entirely in this village since Mulcair took to drawing teeth; and it's according to custom you must go wherever you'll be Patsey Flynn.

PATSEY It's over willing I am in sure to go according to the hang of a place sir; 'tisn't special I wanted to be held but hearing it the custom ever and always. Well, isn't it great marvels entirely a man sees when he travels a while from home; and the strongest and bravest man often having to be held by six and he having a tooth pulled above in Meenscubawn.

JIM 'Tisn't so long since that was the case here till Mulcair turned at it. It's on the flat of your back on the floor you'll be my dear man with Mulcair, he on his knees over you with the pinshers. Was it ever known to you the plan in the wide world to beat that?

PATSEY Oh wirra, isn't it great ingenuity do be in the brain of a smart man? Is it to struggle at all I'll be let meself? Is it the custom here, sir?

JIM A little. If the pain is that severe one struggle is allowable; if it is too severe entirely the second struggle even wouldn't be out

7

of the way altogether, but Mulcair don't like the third struggle at all. On the first struggle you'll get a belt on the right cheek, on the second a riser on the left, but on the third struggle it's a terrible batter he gives entirely. 'Twouldn't be wishing to you to make the third struggle with Mulcair; and 'tisn't right to do it either when the man don't like it.

PATSEY Indeed, it isn't again custom I'll go and to be making three struggles so.

[MAGE *comes in*]

MAGE [*hands* JIM *tin-can*] Would you get the like of that for porter in the town of Lyre? It's only after being tapped that new half barrel is, Jim the Gardener, and that porter is as strong and as fresh as the hour it left the brewery above in the city of Dublin.

JIM [*shaking tin-can*] God bless it! it's a fine head that's on it entirely.

MULCAIR [*coming and looking over* JIM'S *shoulder*] Is the full gallon in it all through?—and it's a little stagger you showed, Mage, and you coming in the door.

MAGE It isn't the full of an egg cup I took out of it then, if I got fifty shakes atself.

JIM God help us Mage 'tisn't clearing yourself you need be and the full of a teacup able to knock you reeling the best day you ever saw in this world. Here! let the man that paid for the drink have the first of it. [*the men drink severally;* MULCAIR *retains tin-can*]

MAGE [*with arms akimbo, looking at* PATSEY] It's a decent boy that's having his teeth pulled to-day and do ye take him tenderly. Don't let it be the case with him it was with Frynk Sheehy and the way he went from you roaring, bawling lepping down the road and over the fields atself ever till he reached his own hall-door. [*she goes out*]

PATSEY [*nervously*] Roaring, bawling and lepping!

CONNY [*racously*] Well, isn't it the show of the world that a woman can't put a leg under her or open her gob but 'tis mischief and annoyance she'll be making for all about her.

JIM [*to* PATSEY] Whisper! [*takes* PATSEY *by lapel of coat and shoves him a step*] There's no notice to be taken of Mage. It's full of jollification she is and it's her delight to be having game at Mulcair moreover if he draws it on himself by making a reflection on her. They do be always reflecting on each other by the way, but God help you if you came between them and they doting down on one another. It's no lie she told about Frynk though, a big oothamawly with his thumming here and there making out to Mulcair where the pains was and he missing it,—till in the heel losing patience, Mulcair pulled two teeth the wrong ones, and letting Frynk up, out with Frynk the door like a cracked man and down the road screeching and making a holy show, my ill-mannered hag that never stood even the one bottle of porter.

PATSEY   It's no fear I'll mistake where the pain is thank God! It's well known to me they are them three teeth and the way they are working me these fourteen days and nights back.

MULCAIR   [*taking second drink and jumping*] Isn't it great life do be in that porter? By jaymini, it's pure griping I am for pulling teeth now; I'd pull teeth this minute with the best man in the City of Cork itself.

JIM   [*excitedly, to* PATSEY] Hurry with you! Now is your time man dear, while that fearful fury and foherough is on him entirely.

[PATSEY *goes on his back;* MULCAIR *comes over him with pincers*]

MULCAIR   [*to* NEDDY] Here!—give us the first bar of green brooms.

NEDDY   [*singing*]
>   There was an old man who lived in the Wist
>   And his trade was in cutting of brooms, green brooms
>   He had one lazy boy, John his son

[MULCAIR *inserts pincers*]
>   That would lie on his bed until noon, gay noon
>   That would lie on his bed until noon.

[MULCAIR *raises* PATSEY *to a sitting posture with pincers; pincers slips and* PATSEY *falls back on floor his head bumping.* MULCAIR *re-inserts pincers*]

NEDDY   [*singing*]
>   The old man arose and he stood on the floor
>   And swore he'd set fire to Jack's room, gay room
>   If he didn't arise and sharpen his knives
>   And go to the wood to cut brooms, green brooms
>   And go to the wood to cut brooms.

[MULCAIR *raises* PATSEY *as before with similar result*]

JIM   'Tis some sign of blood he is showing, Mulcair.

MULCAIR   Psh! 'tisn't even a sign atself you could call that little tint [*inserts pincers*]

9

JIM 'Tis hardly a sign then, I suppose.

NEDDY [*singing*]

> John he arose and he tore on his clothes
> And he stood on the floor with fame, brave fame
> Saying—a man of my blood and learning so good
> Must I humble down to cut brooms, green brooms
> Must I humble down to cut brooms?

[MULCAIR *raises* PATSEY *and misses as before*]

JIM 'Tis some sign of blood he is giving now, faith.

MULCAIR It is and it isn't. [*inserts pincers*]

NEDDY

> John said no more but away he did go
> Till he came to the Castle of Fame, brave Fame
> He called to the gate as loud as could spake
> Saying-fair maid do you want any brooms, green brooms
> Saying fair maid do you want any brooms?

[MULCAIR *raises* PATSEY; *extracts tooth;* PATSEY *falls back as before*]

JIM [*ecstatically*] Didn't I know it would come with that drive and the black look that came over you Mulcair and your tongue out. But it was a great holt you had of it and it a fine sound tooth atself. It's them stumps that do ever and always put you to the pin of your collar to make the right job of Mulcair, like the night you were at Michaeleen Quirke.

MULCAIR [*flinging tooth to* CONNY] Wrap that up in a piece of paper, let you.

JIM Would you say it's a share of blood he's showing now, Mulcair?

MULCAIR [*after some reflection*] Well, you might call it a little share.

JIM Amirra, I'm thinking Michaeleen Quirke gave more blood after the first miss than this man after three, tooth pulled and all.

MULCAIR He did indeed,—and twice. [*inserts pincers*]

PATSEY Oo! wow-wow-wow! [*struggles*]

MULCAIR [*slapping him on right cheek*] Be quiet, will you? [*slapping him on left*] Be quiet, will you again?

[PATSEY *ceases struggling*]

NEDDY [*singing*]

> The lady being high and John cast an eye
> John's beauty put her in game, brave game
> She called to her maid as loud as could spake
> Saying bring me on bonnie lad with his brooms, green brooms

JIM   Ha! didn't I know if it was as firm in him as the hobstone of hell atself you'd bring it in that drive Mulcair.

MULCAIR   [*flings tooth to* CONNY] Wrap that up, let you.

JIM   Could that be great blood now, Mulcair? It is coming through his ears now in style faith,—little less than is coming through his mouth and nose, atself.

MULCAIR   [*somewhat doubtfully*] Well, it is great blood I suppose, in a way.

PATSEY   Oo! wow-wow-wow!

MULCAIR   [*slaps* PATSEY] Is it that noise is coming from you again?

[*to* JIM] Bring a vessel till we turn his head into it and let the blood come free from his mouth.

JIM   There is that little bowl?

MULCAIR   Wouldn't you bring that old big battered tin-can in the corner, and there another tooth to be pulled?

[JIM *goes for tin-can*]

NEDDY   [*singing*]
    John said no more but away he did go
    Till he came to the fair lady's room, gay room

[MULCAIR *and* JIM *turn* PATSEY'S *face over tin-can*]
    Young man then she said, will you lay by your trade
    And marry a lady in bloom, full bloom
    And marry a lady in bloom.

[MULCAIR *inserts pincers*]

PATSEY   Oo! wow-wow-wow!

MULCAIR   Will you have conduct? [*slaps him*]

PATSEY   Oo! wow-wow-wow!

MULCAIR   Take that now for yourself! [*slaps him again*]

NEDDY   [*singing*]
    Indeed Ma'am I would and that if I could
    If I had the face to presume, presume
    The bargain was made and John was well pleased
    To be wed in the fair lady's room, gay room
    To be wed in the fair lady's room, gay room.

[MULCAIR *raises* PATSEY *and misses*]

JIM   Well, that's great blood entirely, now, Mulcair.

MULCAIR   [*indifferently*] It is. It is afterwards the great benefit will come to him of giving that blood.

[*inserts pincers*]

JIM   It is in mind of Mary Quilter that remark puts me and what happened to her of a day and she to fall off the big clift in Islandboy. It's thirty years since it occurred to her Mulcair, and 'tis myself was eye witness to it;—by chance;—it's to the town of Lyre I was going and whatever pinched me to take the short cut.—It's misery overtook myself the same day and I crossing Gloshavuir,—a tripull of rushes to come again me,—I tumbled and it's up to my neck in slush it landed me;—but let me tell you of Mary:—the clift is on the way to town,—at the bottom of Mick Donovan's land aroo,—it's well you know it. It was under the clift I was picking my steps—at this side of the gripe—and it's Mary I seen on the pinnacle of the tip-top. It's a great blow of heat came the same hour Mulcair. It's picking fraycawns Mary was. It's the biggest tooth for fraycawns Mary had, I ever seen in a woman, and if it was put before her she'd climb the steeple when the time would come to her for that feed. I looked up and if I did, down come Mary—whatever slip or stumble she made—rolling and tearing and crashing over brambles and stumps and corrigs of stones and every misfortune till she was landed on the flat of her back at the bottom of the clift. I forgot—she let a screech and she starting to fall. Help! said she, and she down entirely. It's to cross the big gripe I had to get to her. Oh wirra! it wasn't an eye or a nose you could see in her but she all tore and scrope from top to toe and she in pure rags. What made the case worse 'twas on the keerogue of an ash bush she landed and seven inches of it was drove through her leg. I never seen that pig killed give the blood Mary gave that day. But—it's alluding I am you now—the devil a harm it did her.

MULCAIR   [*contemptuously*] Ptse!—it did I'm sure.

JIM   Faith, it's herself told me a fortnight after that she was never in better wind in her life and she healed up. But it's sound people the Quilters were from stem to stern, and it's great tasby was someway in that clan.

CONNY   [*bitterly*] Bad luck to them!—it's too much tasby was in them, the pack of thieves and rogues.

MULCAIR   Up with the last bar of Green Brooms!

NEDDY

> So gentlemen drink and say what you think
> There's no trade like the cutting of brooms, green brooms
> Above all other trades from the East to the West

There's no trade like the cutting of brooms, green brooms
There's no trade like the cutting of brooms!

[MULCAIR *pulls* PATSEY *to his feet; wheels him around floor with pincers*]

JIM [*claps his hands*] Oh, isn't this the greatest marvel ever seen in the wide world!

CONNY [*gleefully*] Wheel him Mulcair;—wheel him you devil!

NEDDY Bring that tooth and it's the finest poem I ever penned will be made on Mulcair the smith.

JIM Ha! it's getting savage he is. I'll engage it won't surpass Mulcair with the help of God! Don't ever let it be said it surpassed you Mulcair to bring the tooth in that drive! [MULCAIR *twists* PATSEY *about furiously*]

JIM and NEDDY and CONNY Good man Mulcair! Hold him!

[MULCAIR *extracts tooth;* PATSEY *falls back against wall with a thud*]

MULCAIR [*goes to tin-can*] Is there any sup left in it. It's never more I wanted it and I pouring sweat.

JIM [*raises up* PATSEY] It's cured you are now entirely, thank God, what harm if you have a little megrum, or buzzing, or a little pain in the head atself. A man can't have everything the way he wants it, and it needn't be making too much trouble for you if there's a little soreness somewhere.

PATSEY [*speaks with difficulty*] It's no soreness I feel. A little light in the head,—a little giddiness. Don't be thinking for a minute it's bothering me that is. It's grateful I am indeed to the great man I came to, but it's above in Meenscubawn I'll be talking of him, Mr. Hogan.

JIM A glass of whiskey would put great spirit in you now for the journey. It's only tuppence I have here or it's a move we'd be making to Miss Clancy's.

CONNY I have fourpence.

NEDDY And here is ditto. There's sevenpence halfpenny here, but three pence halfpenny of that is wanted for an ounce of tobacco; and what's tenpence between five of us?

PATSEY [*searching his pockets*] Thank God! if it isn't elevenpence I have in coppers.

JIM It's as right as paint we are now and rise up, Neddy.

MULCAIR [*jumps*] Them teeth is the finest job I ever done; it's lepping out of my skin I am Jim the Gardener.

JIM [*slaps* PATSEY *on back*] Was he ever known to you the like of Mulcair, the smith? There was never a greater brain in a man, I am telling you; it's the finest neighbour he is, and the best hearted man he is, that ever walked on two feet. [*they all go out slowly*]

CURTAIN

The Country Dressmaker

IN THREE ACTS

First printed in FIVE PLAYS, Dublin 1914

CHARACTERS

Julia Shea, *a country dressmaker*
Norry Shea, *her mother*
Matt Dillane, *their neighbour*
Min, *his daughter*
Michael Clohesy, *a strong farmer*
Maryanne, *his wife*
Babe
Ellie } *their daughters*
Jack, *their son*
Pats Connor, *a returned American*
Luke Quilter, *the man from the mountains*
Edmund Normyle

PLACE

Norry Shea's kitchen, first and third acts; second act, Michael Clohesy's kitchen. (The first and second acts occur on the same day; the third act after an interval of three weeks.)

The Country Dressmaker

ACT I

The scene takes place in the interior of Norry Shea's kitchen. At left is the entrance door. Window at right of door. Small deal table under window. Dresser at left. Fireplace at right. Julia Shea is seated on sugan chair right of table, reading a novelette. She puts it down, takes a photograph out of a small box on table, and looks at it.

JULIA   When I do look at his likeness, I do be ashamed of the little doubts that come to me of late. But how can I help them and the way you are all reflecting on Pats and set on my marrying Edmund Normyle? Ah, God knows what struggles Pats has in Pittsburgh to make that pile he writes about to the Clohesys. [*takes up novelette*] Lady Gwendolen, how true she was to Sir Geoffrey, and all the temptations that came her way! She had a sound and loyal heart. [MIN DILLANE *comes in unperceived*] Still, she never thought more of him than I do of Pats. Ah, Pats, Pats, the wide world hasn't the equal or the likes of you, Pats Connor.

MIN   Well, Julia Shea, you're the show of the world with that old likeness, gaping and moaning over it these seven years and more.

JULIA   Min Dillane, it's very abrupt you are entirely. [*Pause*] If you only knew what it was to have the right love. If you had only known Pats Connor!

MIN   [*yawns*] Some say he was a vain little fellow, then, a little dandy, as proud of his curls as a peacock. 'Twas said he used the curling-tongs itself on a pattern day or going to a dance.

JULIA [*shakes head*]   Backbiters! 'Twasn't in need of the curling-tongs he was, the curls fell in pure little natural waves down on his forehead, and he used always wear the cap back on his poll.

MIN   Psough! I never like to see curls on a boy. [*sits at table*]

JULIA [*replacing photograph in box*]   There are curls and curls. If I could describe to you Pats's!

17

MIN It's all one. Curls or no, people once they go away are never the same again. The like of your love and faith was never seen to be having hopes of him all these years, the way he has acted and all.

JULIA You are all of one mind, all down on him, and the wide ocean is between us. 'Twas the same with Sir Geoffrey. 'Twas the hard word they had on him, and the aunt setting them on, and she wanting Gwendolen to marry that black-hearted Lord Maltravers. But she stuck to him for twenty years, and she not knowing what became of him in foreign parts. [*showing paper to* MIN] There's the picture where he's holding her in his arms after coming back. The villain, Lord Maltravers, is going out the parlour door, and it's a terrible look he's giving Gwendolen and Sir Geoffrey. I'm done with it, and you can take the paper now to your mother.

MIN [*after a pause*] That's a wonderful tall man, and he dressed out in the 'sut' that's letting the fellow out the door with the hump. They don't know he's there at all, and the way they are clapped up to one another in the middle of the floor. [*turns over pages*] Julia, you must have a great head, and to be reading all this print in the *Family Reader*. In five minutes my eyes would be swimming, and it's like a megrum would come in my head. [*folds paper*] You have mother as bad as yourself over it—her eyes streaming for a full half-hour over the lady in the last number that smothered herself in the rushes and slush.

JULIA Poor Inez! It's more sinned against than sinning she was. Min, 'twas the saddest thing I ever read to have her go and drown herself in the dark water, and the night winds whistling through the reeds.

MIN Oh, Julia, isn't it a great brain you have entirely itself, and to be keeping all that in your head? 'Twas 'reeds' not 'rushes', mother read out in sure. [*pause*] Still, Michael Mick Ned says he wouldn't give a pin's point for all that's in the *Family Reader,* but he'd swear by the Budget and all the murders and fine newes and things that do be in it.

JULIA Hesht! Is that your father's voice I hear? [*rises and looks out window*] It's calling to my mother he is, and she coming up the path with the costerwaun for the hens.

MIN He'll be coming in, Julia. I'm thinking he'll be wanting you to make up your mind over Edmund Normyle this evening.

JULIA Min Dillane, it's distracted I am; it's distracted I am entirely.

Why can't they leave me go my own way? Why should Matt Dillane be carrying on like this. What does the effing man want anyhow?

MIN   Why then, Julia, it's the staunch friend he is to your mother and yourself.

JULIA   'Tisn't a word I'd be saying against him: I'd walk on my knees to serve him if he wasn't so impatient in himself.

MIN   'Tis for your good he is. They'll be in on us. I hear them saluting. [*rises*] Well, I wouldn't be staying here talking like a boolumshee. I only came hither for my blouse for myself.

JULIA   Min, don't be wild with me. There's a few stitches yet wanting to it. I'll finish it if I have to wait up till dawn to have it in time for you for the Races. I had to do that dress for Ellie Clohesy or she'd have my life.

MIN   Oh, I'll engage the Clohesys will always get the best of it, and there's nothing thought of the next-door neighbours. It's the people far away . . .

JULIA   Here's Matt Dillane, here's your father coming. Come up in the room and try on the blouse again, Min, till we see how it looks on you in the daylight. [*they go into room.* NORRY SHEA *followed by* MATT DILLANE *comes in; she empties apron of costerwaun near dresser*]

MATT   No, Norry Shea, though Edmund Normyle is a friend to me from the Ahern woman itself, it's a long sight better I think of you and your daughter. Twenty years we have been near neighbours, and a bad word hasn't passed between us. I was so ashamed before the people I had to speak to Edmund Normyle to bring him to some resolution; and let the blame be on herself if she lets him go and he comes over this threshold no more. That's if he has the spunk now itself, the booby, to keep away from her.

NORRY   He do be hoping all and all along that she'd change in the end, Matthew.

MATT   Psough! If he had any spirit in him she might think something of him, but he craving and craving of her week in week out these three years. I do be prancing above in the haggard when I see him coming along sneaking and stealing over the bounds ditch! I do be wild! I'd like to give him a kick!

NORRY   There isn't a turn in her, Matthew, unknown to me, and times of late it comes before me she's softening towards Edmund Normyle.

MATT She has taken a long day to consider over it. Well, now, was there ever the likes of this woman seen on the face of the globe, waiting on her own hearth for this man, Pats Connor, that's gone out of her sight for ten years, and she not knowing for a surety what canter he is on at all?

NORRY Don't blame her, Matthew. It's grew into her from pondering. God forgive me, but she thinks there's something . . . [*pause*] something wonderful in Pats Connor.

MATT There is! If there was plain good in him itself! But he showed his kidney, and the return he gave you, and he fed out of your house after he being thrown on the world an orphan. I'll engage it isn't a five-pound note he'll send you of a Christmas.

NORRY He sent but one pound and a letter to myself the first year he went.

MATT According to their own account, he writes to the Clohesys, the big people, though it was a hard do of it he had with Michael the year before he left for America, connections though they were itself.

NORRY They are the sorrowful Clohesys to us. If they kept the newes and photographs they get from him to themselves, 'tis long ago she'd have the thought of Pats Connor out of her head.

MATT Misfortune followed whoever had dealings with the Clohesys. There's a bad strain in them wherever they came from the first day. But let me speak easy. They're a big clan now in the parish.

NORRY It's no gainer she is by the Clohesys, Matthew. She don't get paid a quarter for what work she does for them. She loses custom by leaving others back for their sake, if a Sports or Races is coming on, little as she gets to do now, the people are so hard to be pleased and they all running to the town dressmakers.

MATT Aren't Babe and Ellie the finest people in the world by her, and why should she charge them? Don't she get newes?

MIN [*coming out of room*] I could nearly hear what you were saying, father, and as high as you spoke once.

MATT That you mightn't hear worse, then, between this and the day you'll be married!

NORRY Is Julia above?

MIN Leave her alone for a while. She's just started to put the last stitch in Ellie Clohesy's skirt. Let her finish it while she's at it till she'll be fresh to go at my blouse to-night. Here's Edmund Normyle and a stranger, and they coming over the field. From what I know 'twill be no joke to make this match, I'm thinking.

NORRY 'Twill be a terrible thing, Matthew, if herself and Edmund part for good. The roses will soon fade from her two cheeks, my lovely girl, and will she leave a good man go by the door?

MATT We'll hope she'll show some splink now that it is coming to a finish.

NORRY This will be a sorrowful day, I'm thinking. Not one of my name was ever in the Workhouse, not one of the Driscolls of Knockanasieg. But it is foreshown to me these months and years that I'll bring disgrace on my name, that I'll get a pauper's funeral, Matt Dillane.

MATT You're a hardy woman yet, Norry Shea, and didn't I think you had a deal more faith! Come now, put a good face on it, and let us reason cases plainly and sharply with her. [*pause*] There's one thing troubling me; this man he is bringing with him from the mountains to argue her, this Luke Quilter, that he has all the faith in, is not a suitable person, I'm thinking. She is too refined a woman to be cross-hackled by a mountainy man, that's used to a different class, and it's stomached she'll get at his play-acting. That would give her an excuse not to listen to us at all, and it would be the same old story again with that creature of a boy.

NORRY The mountainy man might have some way with him, Matthew. He can do no harm and the way we are. He might put reason into her and let us be patient.

[LUKE QUILTER *and* EDMUND NORMYLE *come in*]

LUKE [*at door*] God bless the woman of the house! [*they shake hands*] Put the hand there, brown Matthew. My dear man, it isn't a grey rib you have in the whisker and you turned sixty. And it's as hardy as a jack-shipe you are yourself, Norry Shea.

NORRY Mr. Quilter! Edmund! Do ye be sitting down now. Don't mind that rickety form. Take the chairs, what sparing have ye on them! [EDMUND *sits on sugan chair near table,* LUKE *on chair at fire*] Ye'll be having a scald now, and ye after a long hardshipping walk?

LUKE Look here to me . . .

NORRY It's no trouble at all; the teapot's on the hearth. It's there since morning.

LUKE Pshough! What do strong able men like us want with tea in the middle of the broad noonday? Don't attempt it.

NORRY There's a great shame on me, but the way I'm upset in myself put it out of my head, not to have something lively to put before you, Mr. Quilter, the day that's in it itself.

LUKE My dear woman, not another syllable out of your mouth now. There is no need on one of the Driscolls of Knockanasieg to be excusing herself. Let the night of the wedding be the night of the feasting. But 'tis a queer early hour of the day for us to come match-making.

MATT Hesht, man! This is not match-making in the general way.

LUKE If it was, 'tisn't here I'd be. I now only practise in special and extraordinary cases, Matt Dillane.

MATT Ptse! [NORRY *shakes head at him*]

LUKE But this boy would have his way. He'd be a pure lunatic if he had to wait for the fall of the evening, which is the proper time to go match-making, let it be plain or fancy. He was over to me before I was half through with the breakfast. 'And will you come where you know?' says he; he's shy, and he ashamed to look up. That was at nine o'clock. Well . . .

EDMUND No, faith, Luke, it was wanting fifteen minutes to ten by our alarmer.

LUKE Have manners, sir, and don't contradict.

EDMUND I wouldn't belie you, Luke, but . . .

LUKE [*to* NORRY] My good woman, within the hour he had wheeled hither to me five times again, and the next hour 'twas a case of backwards and forwards with him. I had to be soothering and coaxing him to keep him easy, but in the heel, he panting and the eyes flying out of his head with the foherough that was on him, out of pure compassion I gave in, so we hoisted our sails and down with us.

NORRY The hour of the day don't signify, Mr. Quilter, if it's good you'll do it in it.

LUKE 'Twill be as right as paint, my dear woman, and make your mind easy. I've been thinking the case over to myself all night and day, and I have a plan that will surely diddle her if all else fails. But let this boy here be dumb. If he attempts to open his awkward mouth while I am going on with my capering, he'll spoil all my ingenuity.

EDMUND [*rising*] I'll be as quiet as a mouse for myself. Norry, is Julia above in the room?

LUKE   Let her be where she is and take a smoke for yourself. [*to* NORRY] Whisper. Julia is a bit over twenty-seven, I'm thinking?

NORRY   She is . . . a little. But you needn't be saying much about that in other places, Mr. Quilter.

LUKE   'Tis little you know of the man from the mountains. Don't be having any doubt on my power to persuade this strange daughter of yours, Norry Shea. It's my delight to tackle a contrairy woman. I'm noted for that all over Cornamona. Since I married the third wife I'm like Alexander the Great that didn't know what to do with himself after he conquering the wide world. Peg M'Assy, the poor thing, is as quiet and obedient as a tame duck. But in the two more, God rest them, ha! 'Twas there Luke Quilter showed himself the master!

MATT   That is no way to speak of the dead.

LUKE   My dear man, don't be talking fool:sh. In forty years we'll be all dead and the wind blowing over us. There won't be a whisper of you, Matt Dillane, in Croughderg, nor of me above in Cornamona.

MATT   Leave that aside. I'd like to make one remark. This woman, Julia Shea . . .

NORRY   Matt! Matt!

MATT   Julia Shea . . . not alluding to her notions . . . is a well-learned woman. There is no good in starting a game of hambug and raumeis with her likes I can tell you, Luke Quilter. My intention was, to reason cases with her in a serious fashion, and leave it to her sense of what was dutiful and good. Then let her choose once and for all and for ever, and let there be no going back on it.

LUKE   You have no brain. The worst way in the world to tackle a woman is to put the question direct to her. She can't bear it. You'd be talking of duty and Julia would be thinking of to-morrow week.

[JULIA *comes out of room with parcel. She goes rapidly to dresser and places parcel on it*]

NORRY   Julia, don't be so shy in yourself. But come back and shake hands with Mr. Quilter, and he a great stranger in our house. It's hardly you know her at all, Mr. Quilter, I'm thinking.

LUKE   Know her! God rest the poor woman's soul, isn't she the dead image of her Aung Mag? I'd know her in a fair, and I'd nearly say you were a fine class of a woman, Julia Shea.

23

JULIA Mr. Quilter, a good day to you.

[*she fiddles with parcel on dresser*]

LUKE Come hither to me, my lady.

MATT Oh fodha, this will never tell.

NORRY [*catching* MATT *by arm*] Let him try his hand, Matt. Be patient.

[JULIA *turns slowly around. She leans against dresser*]

LUKE Come, come, my good girl, and don't be distant in yourself.

JULIA Mr. Quilter, it isn't a short answer I'd be making to a stranger, but it's a rude kind of a man you are, I'm thinking.

LUKE [*to* NORRY *aside*] In the turn of a hand I'll be in a lump of sugar. As the book says, when the mountain wouldn't come to Mahomet, Mahomet he had to go to the mountain. [*rises*] Don't be in dread of me now. It's a good gaze I want to get of you, to see what's wonderful in Julia Shea above Bridget Gildea. [*pause, shakes head, laughs*] What's come over this unfortunate boy, Edmund Normyle, and Bridget Gildea all but out of her mind on account of him? What . . .

JULIA Mr. Quilter, 'twasn't to-day or yesterday I advised Edmund to take her and she fond of him. [*tosses her head*] But Julia Shea does not set up for beauty, Mr. Quilter. She knows she's no patch on the strong able woman from Cornamona, Bridget Gildea.

LUKE Isn't it an awkward man I am, and the way I do be expressing myself? 'Tisn't on Julia Shea's beauty I'd be reflecting, howbe the brown girl is the queen of Cornamona; and in the whole parish itself, where's the brown girl could match the beauty of Bridget Gildea? Still, Julia Shea, and you black-haired itself, in the comparison of pure loveliness I'd place you a quarter above Bridget Gildea. [JULIA *laughs*] Only it wasn't to comeliness I was alluding at all, my dear girl, and you taking me short, but to age. Age!

JULIA Age!

LUKE Age! Age! Age is a woeful and a terrible misfortune.

JULIA [*sharply*] I'd like to give you a slap in the face.

LUKE [*catching her wrist*] I'll stop you doing that anyway.

JULIA [*trying to disengage her hand*] It's myself that has worn my age, Mr. Quilter, and I'll thank you to remember it.

LUKE [*laughing*] That's a curious remark for a young woman to make and she in her prime.

JULIA [*somewhat mollified*] I don't understand you at all, and the way you are saying things backwards and forwards.

LUKE It's a young woman you are by yourself, but in the comparison with Bridget Gildea you wouldn't be such a young woman at all. And when I'm thinking of age it's alluding I am to the difference in the years that have passed over Julia Shea and over Bridget Gildea. I was at the christening of Bridget Gildea; but it was plain to me what your age was, and you opening your eyes full wide at the dresser. It's by her eye I judge the age of a female.

JULIA [*tosses head*] Females must be animals according to mountainy people, I am thinking, and the way you reflect on them.

LUKE There's a new light for every year till the day comes when the lights begin to dull. Then comes age, age, age! God help us, there's no cure for age! It's a while you are from age yet, Julia Shea, but Bridget Gildea is in the first flush of youth, hardly nineteen itself; your age by the lights is twenty-three years and six months.

JULIA Well, it's a sharp man you are surely. [*laughs*]

LUKE [*speaking solemnly*] Julia Shea, at twenty-five the spring of life is gone for evermore.

JULIA [*half to herself*] Lady Gwendolen was thirty-seven when Sir Geoffrey came back.

LUKE Now, look here to me. At thirty a single woman is an old withered hag, and there's no more about her in this world.

JULIA Nonsense. At thirty a woman isn't so very far advanced, or at thirty-two itself.

LUKE Muceerough! Thirty or thirty-two! I give up a woman that isn't married for herself at twenty-five. They'd pelt her likes off the streets in America if the Yanks caught her head outside the door.

JULIA [*angrily*] I wouldn't believe that at all.

LUKE The wide world knows the Yanks goes to meet the ships. They call the new ones 'green,' and it's looking for fresh young girls they do be when they goes to the ships. They grin at the sight of a female if she was over seventeen, and she'd want to be Venus herself to get a man and she but a trifle over twenty.

JULIA A girl of seventeen or twenty! What is she but a pure child?

LUKE My dear girl, it's a different view the Yanks take of it; and if a single Yank comes home and he as grey as the hills, it's the youngest girl in the house he'll be looking for. It's strange to me that a woman of your reading should be waiting for a Yank, and the small encouragement he has given you itself. If I was in your two shoes I'd sooner marry a tinker than wait for a Yank. It's a lone goslin' through the world you'll be going to the end of your days on account of him. God help the woman that would have her teeth wore waiting on the chance of a Yank coming over the seas to her!

JULIA [*angrily*] I won't listen to you, Mr. Quilter; it's too presumptuous you are entirely for a strange man, I'm thinking.

[*turns her back on him*]

MATT [*to* NORRY] Psh! Didn't I foretell? [*sniffs*]

NORRY [*catching him by arm*] Matt! Matt!

LUKE [*speaking slowly*] My dear girl, its' the truth you have. Myself and Edmund Normyle aren't refined or Inglified, and we had better be going for ourselves and not to be staying where there's no welcome for us.

JULIA I wouldn't be taking you short, Mr. Quilter, if you wouldn't be reflecting on things. There might be other matters to talk about.

LUKE For what should I be talking when I'll get no rehearing?

JULIA We needn't be speaking of Yanks at all. There's other subjects you could talk of surely.

LUKE We will, and there won't be no crossness between us. It's of love we'll be talking. [JULIA *laughs*] It's to tell you about this man I want. Your heart would soften if it was of flint itself in you knew the way he does be above in Cornamona. When the day's grand with the sun shining above in the heavens he do be in great wind, and hope and joy do be in him. It's smiling like a half-fool he does be to himself and he listening to the thrushes and blackbirds and robineens singing in the little crough below the house, for it's your own voice he thinks he hears amongst them and they making ceol.

EDMUND [*seated on chair at fire, turning round*] I' faith, Luke, and who told you . . .

LUKE But when the day is dull and chilly and the grey rain comes fleeping down Knockroe, he do be lonesome in himself and not a word out of him, he thinking then somehow that your heart is sealed against him and that 'twill never change . . .

EDMUND I' faith, Luke, and how did you guess . . .

LUKE [*taking her hand*] You'd see him prowling along by the ditches, his head under him and he sighing. And he does be fit to weep itself when he gazes towards Croughderg, and no sight of it at all through the drizzle falling on the low bogs. There's no mercy in Julia Shea's heart for him, and 'tis then he rightly knows it.

JULIA But Edmund himself must know the way I am, and that there is no happiness in the wide world I wouldn't wish him. It's an unfortunate world, God forgive me! I will go and sit down now, Mr. Quilter. [*trying to take her hand out of his*]

LUKE [*points*] Look out the window, Julia Shea! Look at he on the bush!

JULIA It's nothing at all I see but a small little bird.

LUKE A robineen; one of the robineens that do be singing to Edmund above in Cornamona. It's to follow us all the way he did, and he hopping from bush to bush. 'You'll have luck to-day, Edmund Normyle', says he; 'you'll have luck to-day'. How sedate he is in himself now, an' he decking his little red breast.

JULIA The creature he does look a stranger. [*sees* LUKE *smile*] I will go now. What'll I do at all? Let go my hand, Mr. Quilter. [*she disengages her hand and goes towards dresser*] What will I do? what will I do? [*pause*] It's my promise I gave, and I said I'd be true to Pats Connor.

LUKE I'll engage there'll be no hindrance to you in a week or ten days' time when this boy will have hooked away for himself. [JULIA *starts and turns*] If you said I'll have him, he's so mad on you, he'd hardly go over the seas, I'm thinking.

JULIA [*excitedly*] What, 'tisn't to America he's going at all?

LUKE Oh, it's no blame on you over it, my dear girl. 'Tisn't you drove him to it, for he hadn't the money to be drove to it desperate as you had him itself. To-day week a card came from his Uncle Tim, and Edmund will be sailing of a Tuesday. [*takes out card out of his pocket and flourishes it*] You might as well be saying good-bye to one another now, as 'tis hardly you'll meet again in this world, I'm thinking. [JULIA *puts out her hand for card;* LUKE *draws it back*]

JULIA Why are you keeping the card from me, if it is Edmund's it is?

LUKE Psh! The card is all right, never you fear. [*puts it in pocket*]

JULIA [*catches* EDMUND *by arm*] Edmund, is this the truth? You to keep it dark from me and you here a Friday?
[*pause*]

EDMUND [*rises*] God knows, Luke, I can't get it from me to tell her a lie. The card is Michael Mulcair's he has, Julia. Luke, don't be wild.

JULIA 'Tisn't he should be wild at all, but she that he has played his tricks on. Why, then, it's one word of the truth has more power with me than fifty of his tricks; and if poor Pats don't return in the meantime, and you'll wait a year and a day, I won't give you the refuse then, Edmund Normyle.

EDMUND It's longer than that I'd wait, Julia, if it was your wish and you fixed it.

MATT [*rises*] Ptse! A year and a day. This is more of the novelette. Let it be finished now, one way or another. It's sick entirely I am of this business.

LUKE Don't be pressing her against her will, now, or 'tis stomached she'll get and she a well-learned woman. Leave it to her sense of what's dutiful and good, Matt Dillane. [EDMUND *sits on table;* MATT [*laughs ironically*] And let her have a little time to be screwing herself to it. Come, we'll make a bargain on the head of it. Let it be three months, and that's neither too long nor too short.

NORRY Do, Julia. Be said by Mr. Quilter, and he for your good.

LUKE There's a cousin of Peg M'Assy's in Pittsburgh and he must know Pats Connor surely. I'll make it my business to write to him to find out the way Pats Connor is, whether he is in poverty or bad health, or whether he ever intends to come home to you at all. It's my belief he has no notion of you, but if he has there will be no blame on you if you wait for him for ten years more itself.

JULIA If I wrote to Pats myself! But I could never do that at all. I'm thinking you'll find out what you want to find out, Mr. Quilter. But let it be three months. I can't be going against the whole world, and it's conquered I am. I'll go now and take this parcel to the Clohesys. [*sighs, goes to dresser*] 'Tisn't going there often I'll be in the future, I'm thinking.

LUKE 'Tis with you we will be and the Clohesys on our way home. [*to* EDMUND] Will you get off that table, sir, and accompany the woman you're contracted to. [EDMUND *comes off*] It's a good distance I'll be keeping behind them and having a smoke for myself, Norry Shea. Lovers' company is no company for a thrice-married man and his day long gone by. I'd as lief be peeping at a pair of hens now, and they pretending to be listening to one another and telling each other the most important thing in the world.

[*whistling heard outside*]

JULIA That hornpipe was always Pats' fancy. 'Twas wonderful the turns and thrills he had for it. No one in the wide world could whistle it like Pats Connor. 'Twas a grand thing entirely to hear him on a frosty morning and he whistling 'The Stack of Barley', and he walking up the frosty fields. [*pause*] But those times are gone for evermore. [*to* EDMUND, *taking up parcel*] We'll be going now.

[*goes out, followed by* EDMUND]

LUKE   It's great power there do be in music, even in a whistle itself. Look at the change it made in her colour and the way it upset her. Well, Norry Shea, as the book says, 'All's well that ends well in the heel'.

NORRY   It's light the heart is in me now, and it is grateful I am to you, Mr. Quilter. 'Twasn't your fault that the case did not turn out the way you wanted it.

LUKE   My dear woman, you don't know me. It turned out the very way I expected it itself. I had Edmund tutored to back me up in the lie, but he being soft and simple 'twas well I knew his conscience would prick him and that he'd say just what I wanted him to say to soften her. If I tutored him to say it, it's a blunder he'd make of it and it's ruined entirely he'd be. Well, God bless ye both!

NORRY   God bless you likewise, Mr. Quilter, and God spare you long! [LUKE *goes out*]

MATT   I give in he's a knacky man in the line of women. The day's spent on me with this match-making, Norry Shea. [MIN *comes in*]

MIN   Norry Shea, it's Pats Connor that's coming home. 'Twas like a Yank itself I saw passing here a while ago, and he going towards the cabin you were turned out of five years ago.

NORRY   'Twas his whistle she heard, and how well she knew it! It's undone we are entirely. Let Pats Connor be what he is, if Julia gets one splink of him, she'll never again look back on Edmund Normyle. [*sits on sugan chair*]

MATT   [*going to door*] Well, there is no use in talking. What is to be will be, Norry Shea. [MIN *goes out*]

NORRY   'Tis true, 'tis true, Matt Dillane, what is to be will be; what is to be will be.

CURTAIN

ACT II

Interior of Michael Clohesy's kitchen. Entrance door at right. Yard door left. Large deal table in centre of room. Large dresser well filled with various crockery. Can near dresser. At right of entrance door some hayforks and a rake are standing upright. Fireplace opposite dresser. Above fireplace door leading to a bedroom. Michael enters with a telegram in his hand. He is rough-looking with bushy side-whiskers. Shouts at top of his voice.

MICHAEL [*shouting*] Maryanne! Is it above in the room you are, Maryanne?

MARYANNE [*coming out of room stiffly*] It is up in the room I am, Michael.

[*comes down stage, putting corner of white apron to her nose; sits on chair facing* MICHAEL. *Hissing like an adder*] Yes!

MICHAEL [*somewhat taken aback*] A telegram that's come from Pats Connor from Cork. The post-boy gave it to me and I going to town. It would be a horrid thing if he came by the four o'clock and no car to meet him. With the foherough that was in me back to the meadow—bad luck to it!—I never thought of it, Maryanne.

MARYANNE [*raucously*] He'd never know of that train and it only on a year. It's only special people do be travelling by it, I'm thinking. Sure it's by the nine o'clock the home-comers ever and always arrive. And put that frown away from you, Michael. I never heard tell of a human being to come by the four o'clock on a holiday from Dublin, or returning from America, or from any other place in the wide world.

MICHAEL That will do, and don't be making a speech on the head of it. Whist! What clattering is that I hear going on in the room?

MARYANNE That's Babe finishing her tea. Herself and Ellie are as bitter as ever with the jealousy of one another as to which is to have Pats Connor.

MICHAEL [*loudly*] Is this the way my commands are being respected by a pair of hussies? I'll warrant 'tis one or either of them will have a mark if it's much more of this cat-fighting I hear going on between them. Let them take good heed of the arrangement to behave like a pair of sweet, smiling dolls for themselves, and let the Yank have whichever matches his fancy.

MARYANNE   It's a wonderful chance that has come to us entirely, Michael, and here they are ready to be scrooging the eyes out of one another if you weren't coming all day and parsing between them.

MICHAEL   It's a God-send it is in sure, woman, and the way we are— a big mortgage on the farm and another debt of two hundred pounds hanging over us because of that bad spec I made in the building of the creamery. It's settled we'd be if Pats Connor has the money we think, and we succeed between us all—and he having no knowledge of land—by getting the big money from him with the mountainy farm and one of the girls. And whatever would remain over after stocking the farm would likely pay off the debt. Then the fortune our Jack would bring into this farm would clear the mortgage. And the other girl to assist in the shop with her Aunt Peg, and take her chance of getting some scrapings in the heel. [*loudly*] Let them take good heed of the arrangement.

MARYANNE   A wonamum they'd both have to go to work, Michael, if this chance didn't come their way.

MICHAEL   If they misconduct themselves before Pats Connor, they'll get the cost for the road, and off they go out of this.

[BABE *comes down from room*]

BABE   Father, 'tisn't a word I'll be saying to Ellie opposite Pats, I promise you, if she don't begin it herself. But I'm thinking if it was a right view you took of the matter, you'd know that one good chance is worth twenty bad ones. When Julia Shea and Pats Connor meet, and he'll learn of the trick we played on her, he'll never look back on us. But as 'twas Ellie kept it up, let her have the blame on herself, and let us tell him of it and not be ruining the both of us.

MARYANNE   Stop, girl! Don't you see your father reddening and the man near his temper?

MICHAEL   If I hear another word of this! Have I to tell you again that Pats Connor and the hungry dressmaker will never come face to face till he's married to which or whether of you it matches him?

BABE   Father, it was only making a remark I was in a fair way.

MARYANNE   [*pushing* BABE *before her to the door*] Out in the meadow with you and be making up the grass-cocks! Get out at once, you mopsey! [*shoves her out of yard door, and bangs door after her*]

MICHAEL   Come hither. I want to tell you about how I got on. We all met in the snug in Peg's public-house—the four brothers and the three sisters. [*speaking in a low tine*] I didn't say at first that we were on for trapping Pats Connor and his dollars. I mentioned I wanted a little favour. I said it wasn't much or I wouldn't be troubling them. I had a little doubt, not being too well off and knowing the way of the world, that they mightn't be too limber or willing in themselves, in spite of all our standing by each other. Do you mind?

MARYANNE   I do, Michael.

MICHAEL   So, before they spoke whether or no, I began with Tim, and reminded him of the time myself and James—um—um—kept him from being boycotted, after he taking the evicted—um—um—farm. How we kept the other man in tow till he gave his goodwill for—um—um—a song, and we—um—um—persuaded him to go to America in the heel. Do you mind?

MARYANNE   I do, Michael avico.

MICHAEL   And then I reminded Peg how myself and Luke coogled the publican into—um—um—marrying her, he thinking she had a fortune and—um—um—she not having a halfpenny. Do you mind?

MARYANNE   I do, Michael agrah.

MICHAEL   I come at Luke then. I reminded him of the time he was a tenant on the eleven months' system. How I managed the landlord for him and I um—um—great chums with Mr. Hobson the agent for—um—um—paying my rent—um—um—unknown to the other tenants, the time of the—um—um—Plan of Campaign. Then I spoke to James himself, how I helped to smooth matters for him the time he—um—um—grabbed Mullarkey's land, and grabbers shot down like crows to each side of him. [*comes round and sits on chair*] I didn't forget Ellen, nor Jane how I saved her, and it proved that she—um—um—picked Larkin's pocket and he—um—um—drunk coming from the Fair. Do you understand?

MARYANNE   I do, Michael.

MICHAEL   We are a great family, Maryanne. 'What are you talking about', said they all, 'or is it to think that we'd renague you in the heel?'

MARYANNE   I wouldn't doubt the Clohesys.

MICHAEL   I told them I was a bit shy in myself, being the eldest of the Clohesys that had most at the start but least in the heel of the hunt, though strangers didn't know that. Then I told them about the Yank and all to that, and how I wanted to bring him here and there among them and they big people, J.P.'s, District Councillors, Publicans, and so forth, till it would get stuck in him how fine and wealthy they were, and he'd never suspect me being dragged, him they all to be palavering of course. They all agreed in one yell. That was all I asked at first. Do you mind?

MARYANNE Ay, Michael.

MICHAEL Then came the chief point. That he'd have to get lashings of drink wherever he'd go till he was bothered. [*pause*] I showed them the telegram, twelve words for sixpence, and just twelve in it—'You see he has an eye for the halfpence', said I to them, Maryanne.

MARYANNE I . . . see.

MICHAEL 'That's a bad sign', said Luke, 'for maybe the man don't drink if he's such a hag'. 'There never was a Yank', said I, 'that wouldn't drink the ocean dry if he got it for nothing. Pour it down his throat', said I 'and I'll pay for as much as I can of it as we go along, unknown to him'. 'You won't pay as much as one farthing', said they all, till you have him nabbed as round as a hook'.

MARYANNE The finest people in the world are the Clohesys.

MICHAEL And Peg herself spoke manly enough. 'Bring him to me, Michael', says she. 'Bring him for six months if you like', says she, 'and I'll warrant he won't go to bed sober a night in the week.' We are great people; we are smart people, Maryanne.

MARYANNE And smartness was never more wanting than now, Michael. The people are not half so simple as they were the time before the agitation.

MICHAEL Psh! 'Twill take a few generations more of the mean things are now rising to ketch up with the intellects of the Clohesys. [*rises*] Well, it's a great ease to have that part of the business settled. Whisper—but don't have a word of this . . .

MARYANNE Mum, Maryanne is enough.

MICHAEL Pats Connor married a strange woman. It's entrapped he got by her and he but a couple of years over. It's a German woman he married.

MARYANNE [*jumps off chair, knocking it down, her arms swinging, appearing as if she were going to collapse. Screaming*] Michael! Michael! Oh, my heart, Michael!

MICHAEL Don't be screeching at the top of your voice, woman. 'Twas as a secret I got it from one Tomaus Brack of Meenscubawn

33

that's just come home from America, and we in Peg's snug last night. The German woman was no great things in any way you'd take her, Maryanne. But it was a queer thing itself happened to her in the heel. [*scratches head*] Wait, now—to tell the truth it's half-bloused I was, and Tomaus telling it to me in the snug.

MARYANNE   There's never a time you go into that snug that you don't get half-bloused, Michael.

MICHAEL   I hadn't a deal taken then, about eight pints and a bottle. Ah, here's what occurred to her. She ate too much of them sausages, she drank too much of that beer, she sat in the chair for herself opposite the fire—she dozed, she woke up, and she kicked.

MARYANNE   Kicked?

MICHAEL   As stiff as a bar of iron.

MARYANNE   Oh, well, if she's dead!

MICHAEL   Let no one hereabouts get a hint of it, but it's up with the break of day you must be, and away with you on the horse and car to Meenscubawn. You couldn't be too cautious in dealing with Yanks, woman. It's twenty times that man might be married for himself since, unbeknownst. Tomaus must know, and the sister would pick it out of him if you could come around her at all.

MARYANNE   My hand to you, 'tisn't wanting for soft talk she'll be if I can work her.

MICHAEL   Take a good quart of special with you and you passing Peg's.

MARYANNE   A pint wouldn't be a bad thing, Michael.

MICHAEL   You'd lose a cow for the price of a paper of salts! Get a quart. And it's a few little trumperies you might buy also for the sister's child. A thing like that would melt her in a hop.

MARYANNE   I'll take a bugle and a rattler. That's what I'll take.

MICHAEL   That will do. Let us out to the meadow now. All the help will be wanted to rise that streak of hay this evening. [MARYANNE *rises.* MICHAEL *searches pockets*] Where in the world did I put that pipe? [*takes papers out of pocket and flings them on table, then crosses to fire, feels on mantelpiece*]

MARYANNE   I was going to take out this tin can of sour milk to the men, but sure if they ask for it Babe or Ellie can come for it. [*goes towards yard door, turns and sees papers on table*]

MICHAEL   That's a show where that pipe is gone to. Oh, it's here. I have it. [*takes it out of waistcoat pocket and lights it. Crosses and takes rake from behind door*] A tooth out of the rake! A man can't put his foot outside the door but there'll be harm done in him! Which of you did it and how did you do it? You do be half mad, you women, when you're put about. You can't keep but the one thought in the head at the time. [MARYANNE *goes out; he shouts*] I'll engage it's one of you hit the sow with it, and if you're bent on hitting the sow you'd fling a gold watch as ready as you'd fling a rake. [*exit yard door, slamming it. Pause.* PATS CONNOR *and* BABE *appear at doorway*]

BABE [*speaking outside*] Cush! cush! Ah. bother to ye for hens and ye fed half an hour since itself. I'll pull the heads off ye, and the temper I'm in after they sending me for the milk. [*coming in*] And Ellie half idle and she raking around the flowers for herself.
[*sees* PATS; *stands*]

PATS Miss Clohesy, I presume.

BABE An, 'tisn't Pats Connor at all, and look at the cut of me in my old clothes. Welcome, welcome! [*shakes hands*] Isn't it well it was myself after all and not old Ellie they sent for the milk. You can't say whatever but 'twas I was the first to bid you welcome. In one look I knew you, Pats, by the suit of clothes and the gold watch and chain. I'm Babe; it's distracted they'll be entirely to hear you came by the wrong train with no one before you, and you going to the expense itself, maybe, of hiring a side-car all the ways here.

PATS Guess I hired no side-car, could see no side-car, and just took a fancy for a tramp like over these rural fields hithermost. Left baggage at railway depot yonder. Turned right into Mullarkey's saloon. Why, they didn't know what was a cocktail! They retail beastly black stuff. Ugh!

BABE 'Twas a pity you didn't make your way to Aunt Peg's. Aunt Peg's is noted all over the globe. Oh, that milk, bad seconds to it, Pats; it's back in the meadow I'll have to be taking it to the men. I'll hang the kettle first. [*goes to fire and hangs kettle*] Pats, when I give the word that you're returned it's trampling each other to death they'll be, father and mother and Jack and Ellie, to see who'll be foremost to welcome you home!

PATS I reckon I'll be real glad to have a shake with them all. Your mother is the only connection I have hereabouts, Babe Clohesy, and I'll just weather it a while in this here rising ground. Rather strange, Babe, that I am fixed to settle down in the finish as a farmer. Guess they have caught me likewise, those old fields and valleys and rivers. [*sentimentally*] 'Twas little I thought it. How I used to scorn the softheads who scraped and starved, all to come back, to come back!

BABE [*slyly, smiling*] Maybe 'tis more than the fields and rivers were calling to you to come back, to come back, Pats, over the ocean wave!

PATS [*musingly*] Ah, there are changes since I last camped in this here neighbourhood ten years ago! Those poor Sheas! There ain't no trace of that cabin of theirs where it stood in the elders outside Matt Dillane's bounds ditch in Tim Fogarty's farm.

BABE Wisha, the poor things were evicted. Julia Shea is a blouse-stitcher now itself.

PATS Daresay Julia is spliced with half a dozen bawling slobbery youngsters. I call to mind that boy-and-girl affair between myself and Julia. I reckon she got cured more quickly than I did. [*sighing*] They all do.

BABE [*archly*] Take care. Maybe 'tisn't cured she is yet. Take care if the dressmaker isn't sticking to you still, Pats Connor.

PATS That ain't likely after ten years.

BABE [*coming close to him*] She is, Pats, surely.

PATS Well, I'm skeered. After my experience in the States, this is the greatest surprise that could come to me that there was a woman living so steadfast as to wait ten years for a man and he thousands of miles away.

BABE 'Twas Ellie did it with her planning. There's no being up to Ellie once she takes the fit. But she never made tapes till she gave under playing this wonderful trick on Julia Shea.

PATS What was that, Babe Clohesy?

BABE [*with excitement and delight*] 'Twas the cleverest thing, but 'twasn't right at all. 'Tis crawtha you might be with poor Ellie if I told it, and it's a show she'd be making of me. She's elder than me by four and a half years, Pats, and it's a little bitter she's turning in herself. Father and mother would be worse itself. It slipped from me that I'd be having some sport with you over it, and whist! they lepped and hopped . . .

PATS [*catching her hands*] Come, Babe, you just tell me this great story right away. I guarantee I'll be mum. You just bet I will. Rather.

BABE Whisper. It's to persuade Julia Shea, the dressmaker, she did, that your whole study in America was to make a pile for her, make a pile so you'd be able to come home and marry a dressmaker. [*laughs*]

PATS [*harshly*] Ellie told her that? And did she believe it?

BABE Didn't I know 'twas wild you'd be with Ellie, and 'tis mad with myself I am to let you pick it out of me at all, at all, Pats. It was a letter every Christmas for these eight years back she would read out to Julia, with a different story every time, and no letter at all to come from you since the time you sent your likenesses long ago. And 'twas one of the likenesses she gave Julia itself, Pats, pretending you sent it to her special.

PATS Well, I guess the dressmaker ain't got her head fixed on the right place, Babe Clohesy.

BABE That's how Ellie did it. The heads do be always going by them dressmakers, Pats. Julia would be sitting at the fire in a half dream, and Ellie reading away in the corner. The poor dressmaker asked to see a letter once, but catch Ellie letting her have a peep at it and it her own make-up, Ellie pretending to be jealous of any one touching the letters but herself and they all coming to her, by the way. 'Twasn't a lucky thing to be doing, Pats, I'm thinking, for, but for Ellie, the poor old dressmaker would have got a boy of her own class—Edmund Normyle—and the man twice too good for an old scregeen of a dressmaker.

PATS Reckon 'twas real smart and no mistake. You just haul Ellie here to me right away. Guess I should like a good talk with a girl like that.

BABE [*in distress*] Pats! And 'tisn't wild with her you are at all, then?

PATS You just bet I ain't nohow. What a real grand girl! I guess she'll weather it through the world. Why, she'd travel first class even in the United States of America.

BABE But she'd never have the brain to think of it herself, Pats.

PATS Ah!

BABE She's the best in the world for playing tricks, but she'd never invent one for herself. 'Twas I thought of it. though Ellie might deny it in me now itself.

PATS Ah, my sharp Babe. I reckon you ain't no greenhorn. I say, you have got the head screwed right there. You have the brain. You are fifty per cent ahead of Ellie, but you just keep that to yourself. Guess you twig?

37

BABE [*in pleasant surprise with a burst of laughter, very loudly*] Uggay! 'Tisn't getting myself murdered entirely I'd be and to tell her that. [*goes and takes up can*] Oh, the milk and the meadow! What will become of me? It's crucified I'll be by them all as I didn't break my shins running to tell them you're back. [*takes up letter*] Ah, if it isn't your own letter to my father itself that's here. [*gives it to him, archly*] Maybe I know what's in it, Pats, about father looking out for a strong farmer's daughter for you.

[*laughs; runs out yard door.* PATS *flings letter into fire, sits by fire, whistles hornpipe.* JULIA, *with parcel, appears at door with* MIN]

JULIA   It must be Jack Clohesy that's whistling, Min. It's a judgment on me surely the day that's in it to be having my heart saddened by hearing that hornpipe whistled twice itself. 'Twas never before I heard that thrill in it but from Pats Connor.

MIN   It isn't Jack Clohesy. It's Pats Connor.

JULIA   So changed, so changed! When Sir Geoffrey came back there was no change in him but the grey hair on his temples. Can that be Pats?

MIN   He's a proper Yank, right enough. Look at him combing his hair, screwing up his pus to the looking-glass—you're in love with him, but I'd nearly get a fit of croosting him with stones.

JULIA   He sees us. [MIN *shuts* JULIA *inside door*]

PATS   Julia Shea! Well, Julia, it's that pile I have made at last, and here I am the same as ever. [*advances*] I have come back to you, Julia Shea—but is there no smile of welcome for me after all these years?

JULIA   'Tis so sudden, Pats. And . . . I hardly knew you . . . and doubting lately if you were to come home at all.

PATS   So those Clohesys left you dull of it? [*takes her hands*] You doubted me, Julia! But, Julia, don't think I blame you for doubting me. Who is to blame but the man who stands before you, who tested you almost beyond the strength of any woman?

JULIA   Ah, it's the weakest woman in the world I am. And, Pats, let me go—I'm not suitable for you now. You'll get some one a thousand times better to share your pile.

PATS   I guess not, Julia, but your dear Irish bashfulness only makes you ten times more charming. But we haven't kissed yet. Julia, my darling future wife, kiss me.

[*he kisses her.* EDMUND NORMYLE *puts his head in over half-door*]

EDMUND Julia!

PATS Julia, I reckon this is the joyfullest day that has come into both our lives. Isn't it, Julia?

EDMUND Julia!

JULIA Yes, Pats. [PATS *embraces her again*]

EDMUND Julia! Oh, he must be the Yank. She don't know I'm in the world at all now.

MIN [*giggling, to* EDMUND] She hardly knows where she is herself at all, and the fix she's now in, I'm thinking. Well, I'll skelp home, and do you go too.

[*they go out;* EDMUND *looks in window passing*]

PATS Here are the Clohesys. It's away we'll go as soon as we can do it polite, for it's a kind of a dislike I have taken to these Clohesys.

[MICHAEL, MARYANNE, BABE, ELLIE *and* JACK *come in*]

MICHAEL [*shaking hands with* PATS) Let me shake that hand of yours, Pats, my son, and say welcome home! Maryanne, Ellie, Jack, welcome him do you in one breath! Is there a tongue in ye, or is it struck dumb with the joy of seeing Pats Connor among ye all again ye are?

ELLIE *and* JACK [*shaking hands*] Welcome to you, indeed, Pats Connor!

MARYANNE [*shaking hands*] 'Tis well you know, my dear child, there isn't need for me to say a word at all. Don't my two eyes show it, with the pleasure from my heart's core bursting through them? Aren't you one of my own? My grandfather and your great-grandmother were second and third cousins, Pats Connor. The flowers of May or a shower after the longest drought that ever came on the land isn't to be compared with the welcome we have for you, Pats Connor!

MICHAEL Amen, then.

BABE *and* ELLIE Amen likewise.

MICHAEL Jack! Jack!

JACK Didn't I say my welcome to him and didn't he hear me?

PATS I reckon it's proud I am of the reception I have got in this house. I guess it's good friends we'll be always, friends, neighbours and connections. But it's real bad to be taking you from your work this fine hour of the day.

MICHAEL Ah, don't have a word of that at all, man. Let us be having refreshment . . .

39

PATS   I guess I won't be disturbing you now. You'll just excuse me for the present, Michael, like a good man, and you likewise, Maryanne, as I have to accompany Julia Shea down the fields; it's a real important message I have to deliver to her mother. I guarantee we'll find man opportunities of meeting each other and enjoying each other's society.

MICHAEL   [*at dresser*] What is this, or is it my ears that are gone mad entirely? Ah, it's one of your pranks you are playing on us. You come to your friends on a visit, you a respectable man, and in the turn of a hand away you hop with a hungry dressmaker! Nonsense, Mr. O'Connor, 'tisn't in you to do the like. Sit down. I'll warrant you won't leave my house to-day, if it was for the sake of doing the polite by all the dressmakers in Europe!

MARYANNE   [*puts apron to her eye*] One of my own, the first day home with him and all, to give it to say he'd think more of a strange person than he would of his relations! What wrong did we do in you, Pats Connor, or has that villainous girl there come and belied us all to you?

PATS   I reckon, Maryanne, 'twasn't of you or of yours she was speaking. Maryanne Clohesy, dear friend, I'm sure you won't be angered at my going with Julia, when I tell you it's in a real soon time we are to get spliced.

MICHAEL   [*rushes to table and fumbles among papers*] Where's that letter the villain sent us for a humbug? It's gone! It's the robber himself that has picked it!

MARYANNE   Will you control your temper, Michael [*throws him on settle*] and don't be making a show now [*soothering*]? It's only a sudden fancy he has taken, and don't make the case worse. [*turns to* PATS] Pats Connor, stay with us to-night itself, then go down to that poor dressmaker when it matches you, and I assure you it's no obstacle we'll be putting in your way.

JACK   Let the man go where he likes and what keeping have we in him.

MICHAEL   [*to* JACK] Don't be putting in your word. Out of this and away to the meadow with you, this minute! [*pushes him out*]

MARYANNE   Pats, don't mind that omadaun, Jack. He's taken after the Hayeses and is ignorant and brusque in himself.

[*enter* LUKE QUILTER]

LUKE   Julia Shea, what have you done on that poor quiet boy,

Edmund Normyle? He's going like a madman down the road, kicking rocks out before him and lepping. [*sees* PATS] Ptse! Fawnorit! [*aside*] The Yank!

MARYANNE Take her away with you, Mr. Quilter. 'Tisn't we are keeping her from Edmund Normyle, I warrant you. Indeed, it's long enough the pair of them were going together and the people talking.

LUKE Mrs. Clohesy, my dear woman, now I beg your pardon. There was never a whisper about her character.

MICHAEL Leave my house, you mountainy snawee! Leave it, I say!

PATS Well, I guess it's not the stranger that will take away Julia Shea, however, but the man that's going to be her husband.

LUKE And it's a graceful wife you'll have in Julia Shea, Mr. O'Connor. I say that, though she has scorned Edmund itself. There's a deal of fear of him. I have a cure for him above in Cornamona in the person and property of Bridget Gildea. [*goes out*]

PATS I reckon we'll be going on, Julia.

MARYANNE Pats, come back! Will you come back, Pats! [*weeps*] Stay for an hour, stay for a half an hour, stay for ten minutes itself.

JULIA [*earnestly*] Pats, do stay with them, I'd rather you would.

PATS Good-evening, Maryanne, good-evening to you all. [*exit*]

MICHAEL [*rushes out*] Come back, and here's the hand, Pats, here's the hand!

PATS We'll meet again, Michael. We'll meet often, I reckon, often.

MICHAEL [*rushing in*] There's hundreds of pounds gone skeeting down the road with a screed of a dressmaker!

MARYANNE The temper is on him, and come up in the room. Let him get into his fit and let him get out of it.

[MARYANNE, BABE *and* ELLIE *go into room*]

MICHAEL [*throwing himself on chair and banging table with fist*] The devil, I say, the devil! [*pause*] Come down; it's out of it again I am.

[MARYANNE, BABE, *and* ELLIE *come out of room*]

MARYANNE Have hope, Michael, and don't be giving way to your temper. He's not gone from us till he's married to her.

MICHAEL Ah, but this is a terrible disappointment to me entirely, Maryanne. But it's a strive we'll make to get him back. We must all do our best. [*turning round and shaking his fist after* PATS] If we could only get him once again into the clutches of the Clohesys.

[MICHAEL, MARYANNE *and* ELLIE *exit right*]

BABE   I have done harm, codded by that old sham of a Yank. I'll do more harm or something will give. I'll break the chaney taypot; I'll break the chaney taypot [*handles teapot, reflects, and replaces it on little table; suddenly*] I wo-ant; I wo-ant.
[*Bursts out door, slamming it after her. As curtain falls, noise of broken crockery is heard*]

CURTAIN

ACT III

The scene is the same as Act I. When Curtain rises Matt Dillane puts his head in over half-door from right.

MATT   [*comes in*] Where's that mountainy man? [*calls*] Norry Shea! Norry Shea! [NORRY *and* JULIA *come out of room*] Was there any trace of that prevaricator, Luke Quilter, here?

NORRY   The decent friendly man. Not a splink of him did I see since the day yourself and himself and Pats Connor were arguing there on the hearth, Matt Dillane.

MATT   He is decent! He hasn't the word of a tinker! No wonder I'd be mad with the man. A half an hour gone we were to meet at the top of the crough after he getting his new body-coat from the tailor, and he was to call in here first. We had it settled and all, Norry Shea, to go to the village before we'd join the drag at the height of the road, and Edmund Normyle getting married at Finuig at two o'clock sharp. Isn't Luke Quilter a notorious liar itself?

JULIA   Edmund Normyle getting married at two o'clock?

MATT   [*drily*] Yes, at two o'clock. [*sees* LUKE] Ah, it's in good time you are, I see.

LUKE   [*entering*] Blame the tailor, Mr. Dillane. He knew the foherough I was in and sewed a couple of buttons crookedly from pure spite. My respects to you, Norry Shea. 'Tisn't for this wedding that I got the new clothes for at all, but for to-morrow, when herself and Pats Connor will be going to the chapel.

MATT   Are we to go or are we to go at all?

LUKE   [*going to fire*] Give me time to light the pipe itself. You're the lucky woman, Julia Shea, after all you've put of you.

JULIA   It's lucky I am indeed, Mr. Quilter.

LUKE   Tut, you're the happiest woman in the world itself. Though that don't contradict what I said about Yanks, but Pats Connor being different from the great majority of them. [JULIA *goes into room*] Isn't he a fine class of a man, Norry Shea?

NORRY   [*crossing and taking up cleave*] From my heart I say it, then. He is a great man surely. You'll excuse me, Mr. Quilter, to be going out for the turf. It's busy entirely we are as Pats would have the wedding nowhere but here out of a compliment to me. [*goes out*]

LUKE Whisper. Have the reports of his conduct in Pittsburgh come to the ears of Norry Shea yet?

MATT Put the question to her yourself, Luke Quilter. It's glib enough the tongue is by you, I'm thinking. [*going,* LUKE *stops him*]

LUKE Listen to me. Sure all the world has it for over a fortnight of Pats Connor's canter in Pittsburgh, and of what the Clohesys did to Julia, with treble added to the story, and they going from mouth to mouth. They must have got some hint of it here and women coming in to them.

MATT As I said to you the day of the market, I know no more than the dead what knowledge of it Norry Shea has, and indeed when she didn't speak of it to us . . .

LUKE Pshough! I don't know what to make of you Dillanes at all. I'll engage if I had recourse to this house 'tisn't long I'd remain dull of what was in her mind, let her be twice as reserved itself.

MATT I have no blame on her to be reserved in herself. If it came to his ears that they were giving heed to the stories of him, he mightn't take it too well, Luke Quilter.

LUKE If that's her point, there's great credit due to her for keeping such a hold of her tongue.

MATT Let us be going on now. We can smoke in the fresh air on top of the road-ditch till the drag comes to us.

[*they go out.* NORRY *comes in and empties cleave of turf in corner.* JULIA *comes down from room*]

JULIA [*sitting down at fire*] Luke Quilter said I was happy [*laughs*] I am happy, he was saying.

NORRY Happy! Isn't it nearly out of your mind with happiness you should be, and you marrying the man of your heart's love in twenty-four hours? I know, for a mother sees all, that a little trouble has come on your mind for the last couple of days. It's a thing of nothing, a change that comes over all of us when we do be overjoyed in ourselves, like a nip of frost that would come of a summer's evening, and no trace of it with the dawn of the day.

JULIA It won't rise off my heart like that at all. It's a black frost that has come on my heart, I'm thinking.

NORRY How could that be in the turn of a hand? It's some silly thing, I'll engage, and in a soon time you'll be laughing to yourself at the way you're brooding over it so severely.

JULIA Wherefore should I be keeping it from you any longer?

[*rises*] I know what is to be known about Pats Connor, and what isn't to be known is in his own conscience, God forgive him, and God help me!

NORRY   O, my, God help me! Who got a vacancy to whisper them reports in your ears after all the trouble I had making signs to the story-tellers, and they coming in here full of their newses?

JULIA   From Kate Broder I heard it all the time you and me were separated at the big Fair. Long before I got hint of it, tight as you watched me itself. But my pride and obstinacy wouldn't let me give in Pats Connor was not what I thought him all these years. [*going to window and looking out*] It's a queer woman I was to be thinking of him for ten years, morning, noon, and night. It's a terrible thing that I have done. It's for this man that I scorned the heart that cherished me.

NORRY   My child, your future is settled now, and do be contented. Isn't it a good man Pats Connor is, and all he has done for us up to the present itself? He has filled the chest with tea, he has brought the sugar, the meal, and the flour into the house for us, and 'tisn't in want of a skimmin' of butter we are since Pats Connor came home.

JULIA   What signify is his share of groceries to me? Isn't it to make all things smooth for himself he wants with his generosity? It don't make him any the better in my eyes now what he does or what he doesn't do.

NORRY   Oh, wisha, my child, don't be letting these wild thoughts get the better of you. There'sn't a farmer's daughter going into the town of Lyre but is sinning in her heart with the dint of envying you and your good fortune. You, a poor girl! You can toss your head soon for yourself, and you going the high road in your horse and car when Pats buys the Halpin's farm and has built the slate house on it.

JULIA   What's farms and horses to a mind gone distracted? It's happier I'd be on a potato and salt with the honest heart I scorned.

NORRY   Pats will buy me an arm-chair, he said, and I can sit at the fire and do my knitting and sewing at my ease—that's when we are all living together in the slate house. The fear of the Workhouse will never again come before my old eyes. He'll buy the best of stuff for me likewise, and I'll go make a new brown habit for myself to lay me out in when I'm dead, for he don't think this one I'm

45

making is respectable enough. He'll give me a decent burying too, and he needn't be ashamed of me, one of the Driscolls of Knoskanasieg.

JULIA It's the bad treatment I gave Edmund after all his love and devotion to me. A Friday he came here looking at me, to see if I was happy, and he knowing the reports that were going around. A harsh look and a short word were his thanks, for the pride and bitterness were strong in my heart. I told him to hurry and marry Bridget Gildea and not to be coming here any more, and it's to please me he's marrying her to-day.

NORRY It's good and proper advice you gave him, Julia, and he'll be in the better of it with the help of God.

JULIA A harsh look and a short word. He'll be marrying Bridget Gildea to-day, and it's nearly the time now for the drag to be coming up the high road and going on to Finuig. If I could meet him now it isn't a harsh look and a short word he would get from me. [*takes shawl from crook on dresser*] And I will go to the ditch of the road and I will speak to him and the drag passing by!

NORRY [*rushing and catching her*] Julia, you'll do no such thing. You won't go and put disgrace on me and on yourself in face of the parish. You won't go stopping a man and he on his way to meet the woman he's contracted to at the altar.

JULIA I will speak to him that was friends with me so long and wish him joy, and there won't be any sin or shame in that.

NORRY Oh, be said by me, and stay now for the love of the good God above in Heaven.

[MIN *enters*]

JULIA I will go to the ditch of the road and speak to Edmund Normyle, and don't be hindering me, for you can't stop me, I can tell you.

MIN [*catching* JULIA] Send a message. There's a gorsoon outside and I will give it to him for Edmund, whatever it is or whatever in the world you want to say to him at all.

JULIA Where's the bit of paper and I'll write it! [*writes*] There's no envelope to cover it, but that don't matter at all. Give it to the gorsoon and hurry, Min, for the drag is coming along by the lower road. [MIN *goes out*]

NORRY Oh, isn't it a woeful thing to be preventing the man from getting married and he going to the altar?

JULIA 'Tisn't to prevent him from marrying I want, but we will part as we should have parted, good friends entirely.

NORRY I don't know what it is you are at, or what you are after I don't know. You that were so modest in yourself, is it you above all the women in the wide world that would go bolder to work than even the females in on the flags of the bad cities.

[MIN *comes and stands at doorway*]

MIN Julia, you'll be made a scandal of! There's a funeral of people on the road, wherever they rose out of, and it's in the middle of them the gorsoon is landed.

NORRY Oh, wisha, wisha, wisha!

MIN They are reading the writing, I'm thinking, for you'd hear a laugh coming with the wind.

NORRY It's the price of her to be shamed after what she has done, Min Dillane.

MIN It's my father and Luke itself that are walking up to the crowd.

JULIA Let the people be going on and saying what they like. It's nothing out of the way I have done to blush for.

[*goes to window and looks out.* MIN *turns round*]

MIN Whatever has cracked into their heads, my father and Luke haven't joined the drag at all, but are talking on the road for themselves. The gorsoon made a pass to give it, but I'm thinking it's my father that stopped him and gave him a slap in the ear likewise, for the gorsoon is racing down home now and he roaring.

JULIA What right had your father to do that? I'll run up the fields Where's my shawl? Let me go quickly. [*rushes towards door*]

MIN [*stopping her*] Don't mind it. The last car is gone like the wind over the height of Doon. [JULIA *half falls against table*]

NORRY [*going to* JULIA] God help me with her! Julia, will you go and sit down on the chair itself. What would Pats Connor think of you now, and the way you are with that miserable look showing itself through your two eyes?

JULIA [*going and sitting at fire*] 'Twouldn't leave them now, mother, at the sight of Pats Connor at all, nor at the sound of his voice, I am thinking. [PATS CONNOR *comes in quickly*]

PATS Ladies, good-evening! I reckon I'm not as welcome as the right man, Mr. Edmund Normyle, would be, and it was a tragic thing that the message didn't reach him. But let Julia Shea lay no blame on that little gorsoon, who blubbered right out to me the injustice Matt Dillane did on him and I coming up the path. I reckon it's a martyr to duty he is. Well, it is a strange thing to see Pats Connor coming where he is not wanted. It is a strange thing, Norry Shea.

NORRY It would be a far stranger thing then, Pats Connor, if you were not the most welcome person coming into this house. Don't be taking a wrong view of what Julia has done. There was something she wanted to say to Edmund Normyle that she forgot to say to him and he here last, the time she persuaded him to marry Bridget Gildea; and that was a good turn Julia did for her.

PATS I daresay it was meant to be surely. Still I feel a kind of queer that Julia should send specially for this man and he on his way to the chapel to get spliced.

JULIA It might be a queer thing, then, and the people might think it a queer thing likewise. But if it is itself, it's no apology I'll be making to you on the head of it, Pats Connor, you that never gave me a thought all the long years I was thinking of you. All is known to me, and 'tis better you should hear this from me now than hear it after.

PATS I guess I sort of understand. In learning of these things a change has come in your affections like, and your preference is now for Edmund Normyle.

NORRY Don't think it, Pats. 'Tisn't in the turn of the hand she could change from you, and she steadfast to you all the time since ye were loving childher under the one roof together. Don't be wild with her. It's distracted she is by them story-tellers. It's the like of her that has the greatest love that do be the easiest upset in themselves.

PATS I reckon she has cancelled her love and prefers Edmund Normyle.

JULIA [rising] It is you that have blasted it with what you have done. You have deceived me since you came home itself. It's no hint you ever gave me that you were married to a German woman, Pats Connor!

PATS I swear then to you, Julia Shea, that I would never have gone to the altar with you and leaving you dull of it. I guess I was a kind of screwing myself up to tell you, and that wasn't easy. You ,were to hear of it to-night.

JULIA What are the people saying about other things you did, and that you never went to Mass or thought of going there?

PATS I reckon I am easy what the people are saying. You would have heard what you were entitled to hear and no less; and if it was more information I was to give you, I guess it wouldn't be given because you were curious for it.

JULIA It's only the dregs of a bad life you bring to me in the heel, Pats Connor. I have no more to say now, but God pity me, and the long foolish thoughts I was having of you!

PATS Well, this ends the matter, and I reckon we can take a way each of our own now.

NORRY [*rising*] And is it going from us you are entirely?

PATS I guess it is, Norry Shea. You wouldn't keep me here to be reflected on by your daughter?

NORRY Pats Connor, don't mind Julia. It's bitterly she'll repent when the fit's off and she comes to think of herself. She went through a deal in waiting for you, and she loved you well. Don't take her short in her flight.

PATS I reckon no man living would forgive her if he was in⁹my two shoes. [*goes out*]

MIN My father will kick the stars!

NORRY It's deep in some people the great principles do be, Min Dillane. Though Julia mightn't think it, it's now they're showing themselves in Pats Connor, and the little vanities and follies of his youth fallen away from him entirely.

MIN Whist, Norry Shea! 'Tisn't his principles Julia is thinking of, but it's the loss of his curls she's lamenting. And, as sure as I am standing in my two feet, that's what has turned her mind to Edmund Normyle.

JULIA You can be joking, Min Dillane, but I'll have no denying it. It's more I think of Edmund Normyle now, though it's none of the love I have for him that I had in times gone by for Pats Connor.

MIN It's a pure puzzle you are to me, Julia Shea. Well, but it's time for me to be skelping home for myself, whatever.

[MIN *goes out.* MATT *comes in, followed by* LUKE]

MATT Well, don't be talking!

LUKE Don't be making rack now. Be quiet and let us be soothering and soothering her.

MATT Soothering and quiet! How can I be quiet with this writing to Edmund Normyle in my fist asking him hither for a chat? Psh! Yes, and a kiss and a good-bye maybe! How can I be quiet after what Pats Connor has told us she said to him, he fit to let down tears and the man not easily touched? Ah, let me alone, Luke Quilter!

LUKE I'd be nearly praising Julia for what she did and said, if she don't go too far entirely. It's no surprise to me to see her nearly out of her stems with the stories going, and she a modest and well-learned woman. Trifles that would madden her would make no pains at all for an ignorant woman such as Bridget Gildea or her likes, and not reflecting on them, but as the remark came down, a more ignorant couple never walked into the chapel at Finuig than Bridget Gildea and Edmund Normyle. Julia Shea, it's a scruple if you don't be said by me now. Let Pats Connor be brought in and we'll make spir-spar of this little tooplaish. [*sits on chair at fire*]

JULIA It's obliged I am to you, sir, but there's no good in talking.

MATT If she would only make spir-spar of it. But look at her now! God help you, Norry Shea, and your head white! 'Twouldn't trouble her if you were going with the river. But she's full of her fancies and notions, and it's selfish she is and taken after her Aunt Mag that no one cared about at all. But what are we arguing with her for? Let her go her own way and pay the price of her lunacy.

LUKE She can't soften, Matt Dillane, and she pondering on that German woman. It's the German woman that's the principal trouble with Julia. I'll allow it's a horrid thing to think of Pats Connor being married to a strange German woman, but if it was itself she's no more now than if she was never in the world. It's a forgivable offence, and will you look at it in that light, Julia?

JULIA It might be forgivable, but where's the good in talking!

LUKE That's forgiven, then. Let Matt Dillane be going on, but it's a reasonable woman you are, Julia Shea, though of course you know what's due to yourself. As well as if I was in your own mind I know what's piercing you worst of all—them tales of the way he carried on with with more females after the German woman going. It's them tales that are working you and maddening you entirely.

MATT How ravenous she is to believe all the newses of him, let them be true or false!

JULIA Ah, where's the good in talking!

NORRY From my heart then I can say that I don't believe a quarter of the stories that come to me about him, and if I stood in my daughter's two shoes this day there would be no scruple on me in going to the altar with Pats Connor.

MATT But 'tisn't like her. You're a spunky woman. You showed it the time you made a match of your own with Peter Shea. That might have been a foolish thing and Peter a poor man, but you gave no thanks to all the Driscolls and they big farmers behind in Knockanasieg.

NORRY Peter was a poor man, but he was a great and an intelligent man, and he would have done well by me if the death didn't sweep him in his bloom. Likewise it Pats Connor, a great and an intelligent man, an' 'tisn't looking back on what bad he might have done I'd be and the great points that are in him. I am an old woman of sixty-five years of age to-day, and I hope I am a moral woman, thanks be to God, but if I was in my youth's glory, and Pats Connor and Edmund Normyle stood before me, I know which would take my fancy, and 'tisn't his money I'm thinking of now, for I would choose Pats Connor if he hadn't a screed to his back itself.

JULIA Where's the good in talking!

LUKE I don't credit them fables myself. But Julia has a right to her own opinion, and we won't be contradicting her. What about if the stories are true itself? Crime is bad, but they are divilish plenty that commit themselves. Look at Matt Hogan—that limb from Hell—and the miseries he brought on families! Look at him, the way he does be of a market day, strutting up and down the street, tasby in him, a pair of gaiters on him, daring the people to their face! But who'd up and say 'Black your eye' to him, and he an almighty strong able man? Psh! He'll get a farmer's daughter to marry him in the coming time, and there's things running to him now itself, to pick him up while he's cheap in the market.

MATT What's up with this woman, then? If the like of Hogan will get a wife among the farmers, and we, the choicest people in the known world, glory be to God! What's up with this poor girl to refuse what's fifty times better?

LUKE My dear man, it's to that I am alluding. The whole wrong Julia is doing on Pats is to be thinking of him in the same light as that known blackguard Hogan, and their cases teetotally different. No man had greater temptations than Pats Connor if he did turn reckless for a bit and misconducted himself, after his time with a tippler of a German woman. My dear girl, that would drive a man wild if he was as moral as the priest! I'll engage it's with tears in your eyes you'll be forgiving him, if you'll take that right and merciful view of his case.

JULIA Mr. Quilter, I might be able to forgive as much as any woman, and it is to yourself I will confess it, and you talking nicely. I might be able to forgive what he done and maybe, more itself. [*pause*] But where's the good of talking!

LUKE Now, Julia Shea, it's the whole solution I have of your trouble, and see if you can belie me. It got fixed in your brain after you hearing all about him that his whole purpose in marrying you was to do an act of justice by you after all the time you waited. Come now, can you belie me?

JULIA It don't signify whether or which, Mr. Quilter, and I wouldn't belie you if I could itself.

MATT Could the man do a finer thing? For what should he get a greater allowance, Luke Quilter?

LUKE My dear Matt, Julia Shea is a refined woman, and it's love she'd be looking for and not justice. [PATS CONNOR *comes in unperceived*] But listen to me, Julia Shea, and every word I speak now is from the heart out. There isn't a man in the world would do what Pats Connor is doing from mere justice, if he hadn't love and affection for you, great affection for you, wonderful affection for you entirely.

PATS [*advancing*] And I reckon I can corroborate Mr. Quilter's remarks, even if I am not thanked for it itself. I guess it was often you were on my mind, Julia Shea, in the latter time and I thinking of coming home, and it is a great wish that would come into my heart to see your dear face again, but I was sure that you were married and settled down for yourself, of course. These are true words that I speak before all here, though I reckon it is little I am making of myself in saying them. But let her have the truth now, as it might be the last opportunity.

JULIA [*rising*] I will say it then, Pats Connor, that I am not worthy of you, nor was I worthy of Edmund Normyle itself. It's no great things I am at all. [*pause, sits*]

PATS The beginning and end of it is this, I reckon. It's Edmund Normyle with you now, Julia Shea, and no one but Edmund Normyle.

JULIA [*rises*] No, it isn't of Edmund Normyle I am thinking at all. [*goes into room*]

PATS This is a plain token surely, Luke Quilter, and I guess we have got our walking papers finally from Julia Shea.

[*going,* LUKE *catches him by sleeve*]

LUKE Oh, stop a while, Pats Connor! [*puts him into chair at fire*] Isn't it an almighty hasty man you are in the line of women, after all the capers you went through itself! 'Tis softening she is, I'm telling you, and the two eyes melting inside in her head, and let her do a little considering for herself in her lonesome. Moreover 'tis something very particular entirely I have to say to Julia that I was keeping to myself till the finish. Sit down now, stay where you are, and Norry will be coaxing her back to us again. My dear man, is it the fine reputation of Luke Quilter you'd be endangering, to have it go the rounds that two he had a hand in turned out in the heel with the woman flopping out through one door and the man bounding out the other? Psh! Ptse! Will you be coaxing her down to us, Norry Shea!

MATT [*at doorway*] Allelu! Here they are! Allelu! 'Tisn't coaxing her down you need be at all, I'm thinking, Norry Shea. Isn't it breaking her neck she'll be getting refreshments for her old friends the Clohesys?

NORRY The Clohesys, Matt Dillane! The Clohesys!

MATT The four Clohesys itself! Isn't this the biggest compliment ever done on a poor girl? 'Tisn't sneaking they are to her either, or keeping a spade's distance between one another like brothers going to work or dinner, but it's in one bunch they are, chatting and prancing in a manner that you think it's a foherough is on to know who'd be foremost to have a shake hands with Julia Shea.

NORRY Oh, Matt Dillane, 'tis well you know 'tisn't to honour her they are coming, but you joking through your temper, the Lord guard us! What purpose is bringing them at all! God help us, Matt Dillane! God help us, Luke Quilter!

[*goes into room R.C. enter* MICHAEL CLOHESY, MARYANNE, BABE *and* ELLIE]

MICHAEL Patrick O'Connor, 'tis here we find you, and can I credit my eyes to see you begging of scraggy things, or is the pride and manliness dead in you entirely? There is a crowd of people on the road, and there is a mihil in Dan Curtin's field longside it. 'Tisn't

53

working they are, for they aren't able with the tears fleeping down off their two cheeks from the dint of laughing and, saving your presence, Pats Connor, they having the haycups. Tell it to him yourself, Maryanne.

MARYANNE How can I talk of it and I lighting with shame? Doesn't himself know all and we watching him from the high road, after we stopping the car coming from town? We saw you going into this poor cabin and we saw you coming out of it. It broke the melt in us to see you go into it again before the people, and we nearly fainted. Michael would gallop away, but I said I would and should come to save you and you one of my own, Pats Connor . . . Tell it to him yourself, Michael.

MICHAEL The horse and car is on the road, and come with your own. We'll shake hands and let bygones be bygones. Don't mind the wretches that are putting it in your eyes that I want you for one of my daughters. If I did itself, they are good girls, and there's a fine farm of land for whoever will come into it. But it isn't to that I am alluding. 'Tis to see you respectable I want and you a relation of the wife's, and it's a good rich woman the Clohesys will make out for you if you buy the Halpin's farm.

MARYANNE Ah, come to your own, Pats Connor!

MICHAEL A man of your position, what pleasure have you with these scraggy things and they scorning you itself? Come to the Clohesys, the biggest people in the parish. They will entertain you in their parlours with a heart and a half—Peg and James and Luke —and we can entertain you ourselves with a good fat pig hanging over our heads and likewise a good fat pig in the peckle. You are a smart travelled man, and the Clohesys will give you a shove up the hill to glory, and you will be a great man of the new times. It's a County Councillor the Clohesys will make of you if you will come to your own.

MARYANNE Patsy, agragil, that dressmaker is the cause of all the difference between us. But we won't be thinking of our differences when a stranger shames either of us and we friends and relations. There's none like your own in the heel. There was no crime in that little joke of Babe and Ellie's itself. How could they help it? Fine fresh jolly girls—she a queer person—and it's succeeding with them.

BABE Pats, if Ellie was a saint itself, she couldn't help it. [*in a low tone*] 'Tisn't any hand I had in it at all, but I going on with you, you rogue, and you letting on to be over-joyed!

ELLIE [*hearing her*] Listen to the liar, and she through and fro in it! [*they fight*]

MICHAEL Oh, ye female scorpions!

[*advancing towards* BABE *and* ELLIE, MARYANNE *shoves him back and goes to them*]

MARYANNE Babe! Ellie! Behave! [*tries to separate them*] Will ye not be entangled in one another, my lovely girsl? My lovely girls, behave, will ye? Babe! Ellie! [*separates them*] It's too fond of you they are, Pats. Pats, you will be coming with us now. [BABE *and* ELLIE *catch him by the other arm*] It's lovingly we'll bring you, Pats, in spite of yourself. Come, Pats. If we murdered each other itself, 'tisn't to do on you we would, what the dressmaker has done on you to-day, the most disgraceful act that was ever done on a man who stood in two shoes.

PATS There is no lie in that. I reckon there is not, Maryanne Clohesy.

MICHAEL That's the respectable man, and go with your own. If you gave that scraggy dressmaker the chance—so help my God— it's a cuckol' she'd make of you!

MATT Away with ye, ye interloping Clohesys! Let the case go as it will. 'Tisn't ye will have a hand in the finishing of it.

MARYANNE Leave him, Michael; Pats Connor is coming with us.

BABE *and* ELLIE Father, Pats is coming with us.

[BABE, ELLIE, PATS *and* MARYANNE *go out*]

MATT I'll break your face, Michael Clohesy!

MICHAEL You'll break my face! Darmurra you will! Come on, Matt Dillane! I am no cowardly man, and by the stars above, here's at you!

[*they rush at each other.* MATT *is thrown on heap of turf*]

LUKE Where's the tongs till I crack Clohesy's skull? [*goes to fire. Then seeing that* PATS *and* MARYANNE *are gone*] Oh, the slippery thing! Has she got him entirely?

[*runs out*]

MICHAEL [*rushes to door*] He is going with them. We have him in the finish! We have him, we have him! Maryanne is a great woman. Keep your hold of him, Maryanne! He is shaking his head at Luke Quilter. Good man, Pats Connor. Ah, look at the mountainy bococh catching him by the tail of the coat and whispering lies into his ears! He won't come with him, will he? Good woman, Maryanne. She has him again, and Babe and Ellie are pulling him. Fine girls! Who is that thing running across the field? Min Dillane! That she may break her leg! They are all tearing him. He is going with Maryanne and Babe and Ellie. He's going with them. He's gone with them. He is on our side at last, and so help me! It isn't a screed of a dressmaker will put the comether on him again. Do you hear, Julia Shea, we have him!

[*goes out.* JULIA *and* NORRY *enter.* MATT *rises*]

MATT [*feeling back of head*] My poll is broken. It's shammy that's made of it, and it's near stunned I am. The treacherous villain, it's the leg he gave me. Is it gone Pats Connor is without a word?

NORRY Gone of his own accord. It's no more he will come to us, Matt Dillane. [*sits on sugan chair*]

MATT It's a lonesome evening you will have of it surely. But if I overtake the ruffian, Clohesy, it's a welt for a welt I'll get or call me a coward and a shame to my clan for the rest of my days. [*goes out*]

NORRY [*to* JULIA] You have your will now. You have your will. The dark house behind in Lyre will be our doom. 'Tisn't the friends and neighbours will be about us in our latter end and we drawing the breath, but it's in a cold place we'll be among strangers. A plain coffin they'll make for us, and there will be no thought of us at all and we going to our long home. You have your will now. What is to be will be.

[*sways herself.* LUKE QUILTER *and* MIN *come in holding* PATS]

MIN We have him again, Julia Shea!

LUKE And it's by a struggle we brought him. Michael Clohesy had him pulled up in the ditch on us itself, till Matt Dillane came and flung Michael on his back in the puddle in the dyke. [MATT *comes in*] Come. There's always time to settle cases among honest people. Let ye make the best of it. Let ye make the best of it. It's many a good man's case.

PATS I guess these are my last words. I am willing to forgive and be forgiven. I am willing to make the best of it.

MIN [*aside*] Julia, do be spunky and make the best of it.

JULIA [*aside to* MIN] I suppose I can't be going against them all. But it isn't making the best of it I am, Min, but like Lady Clara I am as the ox going to the slaughter. Not because of the German woman, Min—for I now confess all to you—or any crime he might have done, but because he is what he is and isn't what he was, Min. Love died the first minute I saw him at Clohesys, and my dreams for ever were over.

PATS I'm waiting for your final answer, Julia Shea.

JULIA The spring of life is broken in me, but if it is your wish entirely, then I am willing to make the best of it.

PATS We will make the best of it. [embraces her]

LUKE It's the most timorous job I ever put of me. But it's a happy couple they'll make with their troubles behind them. I have the name of being a jolly man with no trouble on me, but for the day that's in it. That's all as I roved out, and it's only a way I have for shaping through a mournful world. With all my talk, it's many a time I had to make the best of it with each of my two first wives and even with the dead-alive thing I have now itself.

NORRY She has made the best of it. But it is he that is to be thanked for it—the great man, Luke Quilter, who brought her contrite in the heel. And when I go to the church to say a prayer for the repose of Peter's soul, likewise will I also say a prayer for the souls of all his departed, in the morning and in the evening time. They will never regret having made the best of it with the help of God. And she is good though she might be contrairy. And he need never be ashamed of her mother's people, the Driscolls of Knockanasieg.

CURTAIN

One Evening Gleam

IN ONE ACT

First printed in THE DUBLIN MAGAZINE (New Series Vol XXIV
No 1) January-March 1949

CHARACTERS

MRS. AGNES CLEARY
JIM *her son, a blind man*
MRS. NANCY HANNIGAN
PHOEBE TOLLEMACHE *a parson's daughter*

PLACE

Mrs. Cleary's Apartment

One Evening Gleam

The Scene takes place in Mrs. Cleary's apartment in a tenement house in Great Longford Street, Dublin. Fireplace at middle back. At each side of fire-place, a chair. Door at right. To right of door a bed in which the blind man is sleeping. At rise of curtain Mrs. Cleary is seen tucking bed-clothes. Enter, casually, Mrs. Nancy Hannigan.

MRS. HANNIGAN   No change in him yet or is there?

MRS. CLEARY   No change at all. It's the same way with him for the last three days, sleeping, sleeping. He wakes up for a bit in the morning, he wakes up for a bit at noon and again about seven o'clock in the evening. The young doctor is only just gone. He thinks it is only some little nervous fit he's got and that he'll be all right again in a few days time. He'll come to have another look at him to-morrow morning.

MRS. HANNIGAN   [*seating herself on chair at left side of fire-place*] It was only a false alarm you had then about his getting that little glimmer of the eyesight?

MRS. CLEARY [*goes and sits on chair at right*] I'd say now 'twas only some twitching about the eyes he got.

MRS. HANNIGAN   I got a fright when you mentioned it to me the first day, though I was thinking after that, maybe that old Aygyptian doctor you took him to twenty years ago was only talking through his hat when he said that your son would die within the hour if he ever recovered his eyesight.

MRS. CLEARY   The doctor only gave a horse-laugh when I told him what the Aygyptian doctor said, 'All quackery,' that's the way he put it, though I pointed out to him that Jim's case was different from that of other blind people who would become a bit contented after a time, even those that go blind late in life, and though Jim is blind since he was five years of age and he is forty now he never had but one thought in his head, namely, to be able to see again. 'Twouldn't do, 'twas all quackery about that Aygyptian, that's what the young doctor said.

61

MRS. HANNIGAN I 'spect he's right. After all what speciality could them Aygyptians have but going on with their codology.

MRS. CLEARY [*looking towards bed*] He's as quiet as anything now anyway, no trouble on him and as healthy-looking as ever he was.

MRS. HANNIGAN He'll be all right so with the help of God; it might be only some little fit he got from the changes in the weather.

MRS. CLEARY That's what it might be then.

MRS. HANNIGAN If the parson's daughter popped in now what an eye she would give me. She thinks I'm a perfect nuisance. I know what she would say—she'd say that woman Nancy Hannigan has no refayned feelings or she wouldn't be poppin' in and out to Mrs. Cleary worrying the poor woman and her son in a kind of coma there in the bed.

MRS. CLEARY [*smiling*] Indeed it's no nuisance you are, Mrs. Hannigan, but very welcome. When one is depressed isn't it a jolly person one likes to see. I wouldn't mind what the parson't daughter says. She talks without thinking.

MRS. HANNIGAN [*grimly*] She does, I suppose, and she often thinks without talking which is worse.

MRS. CLEARY I find her all right then. She's a generous poor thing. 'Tisn't that I would take anything from her without doing her the good turn when it would be my time.

MRS. HANNIGAN What special virtue is it for her to be on the give and take—don't we all do that. It's only dirt I am in her eyes, Mrs. Cleary, that's the way to say it. 'Twas only a few days ago she remarked to Mrs. Durcan that I was a rale Dublin ould wan—just like one of Jimmy O'Dea's dames from Kimmage. Did you ever in your life hear anything more insulting than that?

MRS. CLEARY She says a lot of things and I wouldnt' mind her if I were you. No pride in her now anyway, though, of course, in times past she would have experiences that we wouldn't have, Nancy Hannigan, being of a different class. That is if she is a parson's daughter.

MRS. HANNIGAN [*significantly*] Now you have said it, Agnes Cleary, that is if she is a parson's daughter. That gay fellow, Gus Parker, the half-gent from the North Strand, would tell you about the flash ladies he knew that would all give out that they were parsons' daughters. [*laughs blithely*]

MRS. CLEARY   It would be hard to believe that Phoebe Tollermache was ever anything like that.

MRS. HANNIGAN   [*sententiously*] I'm not saying that, Mrs. Cleary, I'm only alludin'. It's a fancy name she has got anyway—Phoebe Tollermache, like a concoction you'd make out from a book.

MRS. CLEARY   I think I seen a name like Tollermache wance, in the *Evening Mail*.

MRS. HANNIGAN   [*definitely*] You couldn't. It isn't a name at all and that's the way to put it. Mrs. Falvey that keeps the little grocers shop in Whitefriar's Street would agree with me about her and our so-called grand lady to walk in to her one day looking for a tosheen of tay.

MRS. CLEARY   They might use that funny expression in the small shops in Sligo where she's supposed to have come from, Nancy.

MRS. HANNIGAN   [*shrugging shoulders*] They might and they mightn't. She's a mystery anyway. She goes off in the morning and nobody knows where she goes to. But wherever she goes to or doesn't go to she knows everything about everybody, however the dickens she finds things out.

MRS. CLEARY   [*laughing softly*] I'm thinking you are prejudiced against poor Phoebe, Nancy, on account of those little sarcastic things she says occasionally, out of fun I believe.

MRS. HANNIGAN   I suppose you'd say 'twas prejudice too, Agnes Cleary, if I gave it to you as my solid opinion that she has notions about your son Jim there.

MRS. CLEARY   [*with a little laugh*] A poor blind man! Well, Nancy Hannigan!

MRS. HANNIGAN   They were on a seat in the Green one day and he put his hand on hers—by accident as I saw. If you saw the way me ould damsel blushed, and the tremble that was in her voice a little later when she was excusing herself for going on a message. But, of course, the poor man wasn't making love to her at all. He thought 'twas you were there, not knowing you had moved away a bit to talk to Mrs. Durcan.

MRS. CLEARY   [*solemnly*] 'Twould be a surprise to me indeed to see him do anything flirtatious. And I wouldn't mind about Phoebe. Ageing spinsters are often easily affected by little things. 'Tisn't but she has great sympathy for Jim, feeling for him like I do myself about the tragedy of his mind as she calls it, from day to day and

63

from year to year always hoping, always wishing to see again. I hope you didn't say anything to her about it, Mrs. Hannigan?

MRS. HANNIGAN [*promptly*] Not a thing. Though, indeed, she would well deserve it if I made a scrame of her over it. I'm an oul' Joker maybe, but when it comes to sayrious matters, I never say a thing to make a warnt unhappy. If I don't have something to say to make a warnt happy, I say nothin' at all. That's my motto, Agnes Cleary.

MRS. CLEARY [*warmly*] And a very good motto it is, Nancy Hannigan.

MRS. HANNIGAN Good job for her she didn't hear the snort from the damsel with the little dog who spotted the carry-out and the ugly laugh of her, or seen the wink the damsel gave me. I'm referring to one of those gay damsels with little dogs that do be paradin' the Green.

MRS. CLEARY [*deprecatingly*] I don't know anything at all about their likes, Mrs. Hannigan. Seldom we go to the Green, and except an odd time like the day you're talking about, when we do it's usually on that long bench we sit that you get to after passing through the gate opposite the Russell Hotel. Most people sitting on it are generally of the poorer or working class like ourselves, I'd say, but respectable people.

MRS. HANNIGAN [*gaily*] Respectable is the name for them, Agnes Cleary. That's the bench which my gay, poor husband Dan—the Lord be merciful to him—used call the most virtuous seat in the proletarian section of the Green. [*laughs*]

MRS. CLEARY [*goes to door, opens it a little and peers out*] 'Tis like her step coming up the stairs. She has been away for the last three days and doesn't know about Jim getting that fit yet.

MRS. HANNIGAN [*in hollow tones*] That's another mystery about her going away for three days, every six months or so. She never goes until she gets her allowance, as she calls it, or whatever it is she gets in that big yellow envelope. She'll be in form after the three days I bet and there'll be some rattlin' on that oul' pianner of hers with the wires screechin' that wasn't tuned for forty years. [*darkly*] Brinsmead is the name that's on it, a name I never before seen on a pianner and I often looked in Piggot's window to see the names on them.

MRS. CLEARY I seen it wance on a big flat pianner in the parlour

64

of a gentlemen's house in the country where I was working for a short bit.

MRS. HANNIGAN [*dryly*] Oh, did you! And of course we'll have a song. I had a pain through the napper from her the last time, with her 'I'm so glad to see you back, dear lady', till she nearly burst her windpipe. We'll have a song all right. After the batter we always get a song.

MRS. CLEARY [*sweetly*] I wouldn't say she ever has a batter, Nancy. She's one of them excited sort that a little puts on the go [*closes door*] 'Tisn't her at all after all but that oul' bachelor man that lives on the tip-top. He has a noisy step like Phoebe.

MRS. HANNIGAN [*deliberately*] Another mystery, her fad or her foible or whatever you'd call it about Jim here and she takes no notice of th' oul' bachelor man that would suit her down to the ground. She'd pass him up and down the stairs forty times in the day and never give him the glad eye. And, I don't know but he's a prodestant.

MRS. CLEARY He's a woman-hater. You didn't know that.

MRS. HANNIGAN I did not. But she must know it. Didn't I tell you there wasn't a thing in the world but that dickens of a woman finds out.

MRS. CLEARY 'Tis your crony Mrs. Durcan that told me about it. Th' ould batchelor man was jilted in his young days. He's a Corkman and they say they never forgive a thing like that down in that part of the world. [*short pause. Crosses hands*] By the way, Nancy, you never before mentioned to me this friend of yours, Mr. Gus Parker, the half-gent from the North Strand.

MRS. HANNIGAN [*laughing loudly*] Isn't it forty years ago I was talkin' of when I mentioned Gus. There would be no notice taken of him now and they all gents, but in those days they were all common and Gus the dude created a furiora. Though he wasn't the dude we thought him. He used get his flash suits from a new cheap feller that set up in Mary Street long before Montague Burton or the fifty shillin' bunch who used call himself Philosander the Great City Tailor.

MRS. CLEARY Indeed, my late husband used to get suits from that man. They were cheap and good enough.

MRS. HANNIGAN [*reminiscently*] Gus was the gayest you ever see while it lasted, but he lost his job and then the finery wasn't long

65

coming off him. 'Twas in the month of June he moulted—the wrong month, and the last I seen of him was standing at a corner holding up a public house.

MRS. CLEARY [*reflectively*] The ups and downs of life do be queer. Isn't it a similar case with the parson's daughter or whatever she is. You'd know be her anyway that she seen things that you or I didn't see Nancy Hannigan.

MRS. HANNIGAN [*sharply*] What could she see, Agnes Cleary, that we didn't see, I'd like to know.

MRS. CLEARY Well, she did then. You may be sure she went to Paris and places like that that we never seen.

MRS. HANNIGAN [*shrilly*] Wasn't Dublin as good as any Paris in the days I'm talkin' of Agnes Cleary. Wasn't it given down in Sullivan's geography as the second city in the Empire. Hadn't we the best companies hot from the West End of London. It might be for to keep us loyal for all I know but we had the benefit of them all the same. And when the Moody-Manners Co. would come to the Royal myself and Dan would never miss Trovatore, Maritana and the Bohemian Girl.

MRS. CLEARY Myself or Jim used hardly ever go to a theayter; still we did see Maritana and the Lily of Killarney. The parson's daughter as you say finds out everything, still she isn't old enough to know the times you had in days gone by, Nancy.

MRS. HANNIGAN Whether she does or whether she doesn't what right has she to be waggin' her ould amber locks at me. By the way she goes on one would think I never did anything but charring all the days of my life. But if it came to expayrences—you can smile if you like, Mrs. Cleary—maybe myself and Dan, by comparison, had better expayrences than she ever had.

MRS. CLEARY Of course we don't know what expayrence she had, Nancy Hannigan, to tell the truth.

MRS. HANNIGAN Of course we don't Agnes Cleary, but I know what expayrences myself and Dan had. They might be paid bigger wages now, but I can tell you he had a good job in the upholstery trade and was never short of money. There wasn't a week but we would go either to the Tivoli or the Empire and we went to places that th' ould parson's daughter never saw, in our earlier married days, adventuring into funny places like the Mechanics where the Abbey Theayter is now and to Pat Kinsellas at the back of Jammets, where the ticket was fourpence, but you'd get a big mayjum bottle of stout for half the ticket when you got in. Dan used love that place.

MRS. CLEARY [*slyly*] I fancy a man would like that kind of show.

MRS. HANNIGAN Afterwards we'd go to the Cosy in Mellifont Lane that kept open all night and where you'd get a roast duck or a boiled lobster for sixpence.

MRS. CLEARY [*laughing softly*] 'Pon my word but you did enjoy yourselves, Mrs. Hannigan.

MRS. HANNIGAN See now, didn't we, and I'd like to know what the parson's daughter was doing when she was a young as I was then, herself and her ould pianner. I bet poor Dan knew more about music than she ever did. She's crazy about Gondoliers and Mikados like the Civil Servant Dan used to be arguing with in the bar in the Gaiety gallery, who wouldn't go to no theatre except when Galbert and O'Sullivan was on. Like the parson's daughter the Civil Servant had his uppishness, too, and he used shrug his shoulders and laugh at Dan. But Dan used to say to me afterwards that the man should be put in a straight waistcoat. Dan would prefer the Geisha because he said he would know the aidjum of it, and he'd stick to his guns that Galbert and O'Sullivan were a hotch-potch.

MRS. CLEARY [*resignedly*] Them things are beyond me altogether.

MRS. HANNIGAN Well, indeed, I don't know the tecknikyoo of them either but Dan did, though of course 'twas at the Empire or the Tivoli that we used enjoy ourselves most. Being a soccer fan—he used go to the match at Dalymount every Saturday—he'd nearly break his hands clappin' when Mark Sheridan would sing 'At the foot-a-ball match last Saturday'. I'd break my hands clappin' when Mark used sing, 'I do like to be beside the sea side, I do like to be beside the sea', but Dan wouldn't clap that at all.

MRS. CLEARY That reminds me of my poor Jim—the Lord be with him—he wasn't a bit sentimental. Nothing for him but a 'tec. story. He wouldn't read a book by a woman if you paid him. So your Dan wasn't sentimental either.

MRS. HANNIGAN [*emphatically*] Oh, not a bit! I used to have pity for the more refayned looking girls on the stage of the Empire and the rattlin' they used get from the audience. 'You're wasting your humanity', Dan would say to me, 'every one of them has a skin on her like an elephant.'

MRS. CLEARY I suppose they have it and to stand the racket.

MRS. HANNIGAN   All the same Dan got the surprise of his life
and so did I to see Marie Kendall, who came starring to Dublin for
thirty years, cry like a child on the boards of the Tivoli in Burgh
Quay after the abuse she got for singing a song about being glad to
be rid of an ould man she was married to and didn't like. Marie got
a right suck-in especially as it was what you would call the parson's
daughter class the big people in the stalls that were bawlin' the
loudest at her.

MRS. CLEARY   [*somewhat primly*] Well, respectable people don't like
queer songs I suppose.

MRS. HANNIGAN   'Twasn't that at all. Dan called it a moral wave
and he used laugh at the fright they had about being corrupted by
English comaydiennes. It was the year the Treaty was signed. If
Marie sang a song fifty times as bad now and hadn't a tack on her,
they wouldn't turn a hair. They are all John Bull's now.

MRS. CLEARY   Maybe they were better then and to object to a
bawdy song.

MRS. HANNIGAN   'Twasn't a bawdy song. Myself and Dan that
were used to Lottie Lennox, Lily Hanbury, Vesta Tilley, not to
mind George Formby (th' oul fellow not the present lad), R. G.
Knowles, Wilkie Bard and all them only laughed at it. Indeed after
poor Dan's death when I was broke with four little childer to look
after and had to go singing on the streets, that was the song that was
my principal source of living, the same song that Marie Kendall
sang at the Tivoli—the Lord be merciful to the poor ould crayture's
soul.

MRS. CLEARY   So she's dead then.

MRS. HANNIGAN   I suppose she is—I don't know whether she is
or not, but what I'm after saying won't do her any harm anyway.
Believe it or not but I got a half-crown from a gentleman once, when
I was singing the song one Saturday night outside Dobbyns in
Capel Street. I had a suspicion that he seen Marie cry at the Tivoli.
He gave it to me just as I was finishing up me ould umbrella waggin'
and all—[*takes hold of umbrella and opens it over head*] an ould
umbrella just like this one of yours, and he gave it to me just as I
was at this spasm [*sings, flourishing umbrella and capering*]

> And I does what I loikes
> And I says what I loikes,

I'm single, I'm single again
[*replaces umbrella and sits on chair*]

MRS. CLEARY [*smilingly*] There doesn't seem to be a terrible lot of harm in it. [*noise outside*] That's her now, the parson's daughter.

MRS. HANNIGAN It is her.

MRS. CLEARY Strange, but I never knew before that you were singing on the streets, Nancy.

MRS. HANNIGAN Seldom I mention it to anyone. Maybe there are things a person likes to forget. But there being something derogaytory about it, and it not being so long ago altogether I bet the parson's daughter knows all about it. Hest! Is this her coming in?

MRS. CLEARY I'd say she is coming in.

[*enter* PHOEBE *rapidly accidentally kicking off slipper from right foot*]

PHOEBE [*hopping on left foot*] Blawst that slipper it's always coming off [*puts foot in slipper*] Excuse the expletive, Mrs. Cleary, and also excuse my not tapping at the door before entering. It was awfully rude of me really.

MRS. HANNIGAN [*shrilly*] Get on with yeez, Miss Tollymachy; is it thinking it's in Fitzwilliam Square you are or in the purloos of it.

PHOEBE [*blithely*] Oh, I don't give a tuppenny for Fitzwilliam Square. [*waving arms*] I agree with Horace Bianchon the medical in Old Goriot, who in reply to De Rastignac, said that life could be just as interesting in the provinces as in Paris, that what really mattered was what was going on within oneself and that your whole world so to speak, is contained between the sole of the foot and the occiput. And good old Milton doesn't he tell us that 'Man's mind is its own place and of itself can make a Hell of Heaven, a Heaven of Hell.'

MRS. HANNIGAN Jacky Milton the fuel man in Cross Kevin Street to say a thing like that! Who'd ever think it.

PHOEBE No, Mrs. Hannigan it wasn't Jacky who said it, but it may have been an ancestor of his.

MRS. HANNIGAN [*dryly nodding head*] Oh, thanks for the information, Miss Tollymashy.

PHOEBE But really, Great Longford Street is not such a bad old skin of a place, eh what, Mrs. Cleary?

MRS. CLEARY Maybe 'tis better to be here than in the South Circular Road where they say the people are thrown out when the bed-and-breakfasters come along.

PHOEBE Unfortunately I hear the bed-and-breakfasters have invaded Little Mary Street. So we're not safe. Especially as somehow I think we are just a shade above Little Mary Street socially [*laughs*].

MRS. HANNIGAN [*also laughing*] She don't like anything derogaytory said about Great Longford Street because she's living there herself, Mrs. Cleary. [*to* PHOEBE] Although you know everything, I 'spect all the same you wouldn't be acquainted with a josser be the name of Bert Quinn, Miss Tollymashy.

PHOEBE [*off-handedly, laughing*] Oh yes, I do know him. Why shouldn't I—he comes from Protestant Row. Three years ago he got six months for breaking into a house in Drumcondra.

MRS. HANNIGAN Well then, you might appreciate what he said to an English flyboy presoomably in the same line of business as himself who was greatly interested in the purloos of this locality. Bert wasn't long spotting him and he up and tapped him on the shoulder, 'Say Cockney', said he, 'you're wasting your time in inspecting the purloos of those there premises. There isn't a man, woman or child worth robbin' in Great Longford Street'.

PHOEBE [*lightly*] He must never have seen my curious old black tin box or what was in it.

MRS. HANNIGAN [*caustically*] He must not. I suppose it is in that oul' antique tin box you keep the deeds of your properties, Miss Tollemache.

PHOEBE [*to* MRS. CLEARY] I asked for that so I must try and take it. Really Mrs. Cleary you are too honest for either one or the other of us. Our quarrels may not be very serious, but I'm afraid there are temperamental differences which render a permanent entente cordiale between us an impossibility. As the saying is we are no better than what we should be, and either of us has the very lowest opinion of the other. At least Nancy has of me. It's unknown what she thinks I am doing when I am away for those three days, and she is certain that on the day I return I am always three sheets in the wind. Yet, all I had to-day was two bottles of stout and a baby Power.

MRS. CLEARY [*smilingly*] Well, you're both sober now anyway. Of course Nancy has been taytotal for years.

PHOEBE [*jocosely*] Mrs. Cleary, you are too innocent for this world. So you spotted nothing. You didn't know that Nancy got a cheque from her daughter in England and that herself and Mrs. Durcan had a little celebration in the Harbour Bar.

MRS. CLEARY It isn't too innocent I am at all Miss Tollemache but too stupid. I should have noticed there was something in Nancy's reminiscing.

PHOEBE I shouldn't have given the game away on her of course. But, as a matter of fact I was in the Harbour Bar myself though Mrs. Hannigan didn't see me.

MRS. HANNIGAN [*grimly*] No need to tell me you were there. I knew someone must have been saying things derogaytory about me and sharp, squintish looks Mr. Delahunt was giving me. I wouldn't mind but he being a nice friendly man that attends himself to his customers, 'tisn't like the majority of big publicans that go off in their motor cars playin' golf all day in Malahide. [*caustically*] So, you went in there for a bottle of lemonade, Miss Tollymashy?

PHOEBE [*lightly*] Perhaps 'twas there I had the baby Power.

MRS. HANNIGAN [*acidly*] Perhaps, but I bet you let no one see you. It's the open way with me and you can be as derogaytory as you like about it, but I will say God be with the times when myself and Dan, we were livin' in the North Side that time, used have the fun on Saturday nights in Magawley's licensed premises in Lower Dorset Street. 'Twasn't Baby Powers the women used drink in those days, Miss Tollymashy, but glasses of plain, but I bet we enjoyed outselves, fathers and mothers, husbands and wives, sons and daughters, just as good and maybe better than the top-notchers you find in the purloos of the cocktail lounges. [*gaily*] And then, Mrs. Cleary, hadn't we the added fun of searching the pockets when the hubbies would be gone to sleep.

MRS. CLEARY [*smilingly*] Well, whose times had their drawbacks.

MRS. HANNIGAN 'Spect they had, but things are so contrairy now after those old wars, for some of us anyway, that we forget what the drawbacks were.

PHOEBE Just imagine Mrs. Cleary searching anybody's pockets though!

MRS. CLEARY Indeed I never did, Miss Tollemache. There was no necessity with Jim. Nancy didn't know him at all, but though 'tis myself says it, Jim—the Lord be good to him—was the best man in the world. Every Saturday evening he'd land me out the whole issue barrin' what he'd keep for tobacco and matches and the

few bob for Sunday. Not a drink except on a Sunday, and I was glad
to have him take his few bottles then for the poor man wanted some
relaxation and he hard at work all the week in the Hammond Lane
Foundry. I used have his dicky as white as snow for him, he used like
a good bright tie, a fairly high collar, and he used always wear his
black bowler hat on Sundays. You'd like to see him a half-an-hour
or so after his dinner as fresh as a daisy, as happy as old boots and as
gay as a bee going off all by himself for his little refreshment.

MRS. HANNIGAN 'Twas different with Dan. Dan wouldn't give
you a fig for all the porter in Ireland if he hadn't company with him.

MRS. CLEARY I suppose Jim used meet a pal occasionally but I
don't think he minded someway. He had long legs and was a great
walker and he'd call in to this place and that in his rambles between
two and five. I never bothered where he went at all and wouldn't
know but for gossips telling me that he'd generally make his deboo
at the Winter Garden Palace and finish up sometimes as far away as
the Ivy House or the Cat and Cage in Drumcondra, and in the
summer time—I don't know whether he used take a tram or not—
he'd sometimes take the fancy to go as far as Baggott's in the Park
—if you know where that place is, Nancy.

MRS. HANNIGAN [shrilly, laughing] As if myself and Dan could
miss knowing it or farther than it—Ashtown—and on a couple of
occasions we even struck Blanchardstown. Myself and Dan were
good walkers, too. Of course, we used take the tram when we'd go
to the Pretty Kitchen in Kingstown on Sunday evenings, though
sometimes we'd take a fit to walk back, but then you can bet your
davey we'd have our last little dose at Booterstown, that was also
bona-fide in those days.

PHOEBE Mrs. Cleary, you are sceptical, aren't you, and so am I.
Neither of us can believe that Nancy Hannigan was such a boozer.

MRS. HANNIGAN [sharply] Who said I was a boozer? I used only
take a few glasses of plain to accompany Dan. And even if I went to
Tallaght with him which I did I'd only take the same. He'd take
a share certainly but he was well able to bear it. And why wouldn't
he a well-fed man Miss Tollymashy. We only shamed ourselves
once—through an accident—a pal of Dan's back from America who
had also an English Pal who was taking photos of the five Huguenot
houses in Hendrick St. to force whisky and brandy on him and
forced it on me, too, in spite of my protestin' in a pub in Queen

Street. We'd have been all right if we went home after leaving them, but when we came to Bridge Street Dan would go into the Brazen Head Hotel in spite of all I could do.

MRS. CLEARY I heard Jim saying wance that brandy makes people terrible obstinate.

MRS. HANNIGAN It made Dan obstinate that night any way and what's worse it made him pugnacious, and he was hardly inside the Brazen Head, whoever he see, when he started sniggering and said, 'Can anything good come out of Braithwaite Street!' In a minute he was tangled with somebody and a dame I suppose from the same street got tangled with me, and in the finish we were thrown out by the proprietor. Afterwards he got a terrible fall at Essex gate and nearly broke his napper and I had to hawl him home.

MRS. CLEARY [*sympathetically*] That was a terrible expayrence for you, Mrs. Hannigan.

MRS. HANNIGAN It was, but the worst of it of course was being thrown out of a place, a thing that never happened to us before. 'I don't mind about myself,' said Dan the next day, 'It's for you I feel over it', he said. And that was a compliment, Mrs. Cleary, and a genuine one. He knew I was ashamed of my life on account of it. And I never got over the shame of it to tell you the truth of it. [*tragically*] But there is no use in denying it—we were thrown out of the Brazen Head.

PHOEBE [*laughing*] I'm bubbling up with envy, Mrs. Cleary. I never had any experience like that. What a thrill I should have got out of it.

MRS. HANNIGAN [*grimly*] It's codding me you are now. I 'spect it's itchin' you are to tell us about the doings Mrs. Cleary says you had in Paris. High jinks.

PHOEBE Alas, I'm affaid Mrs. Cleary is under a strange misapprehension. I'm like the poor girl in one of the musical comedies that your husband, Dan, Mrs. Hannigan, had such a high opinion of.

MRS. HANNIGAN [*to* MRS. CLEARY *excitedly, pointing finger*] And you didn't think she knew things so far back as that. But doesn't she! Didn't I tell yeez.

PHOEBE [*tranquilly*] Just like the poor girl in the musical comedy:
Cold, cold, awfully cold, well I should think it was rather,
And a strawberry mark in the middle of my back
Was all I was left by my father.

73

MRS. HANNIGAN [*suddenly catching hold of umbrella, capering and singing*]

> Cold, cold, awfully cold, well I should think it was rather,
> And a strawberry mark in the middle o' me back
> Was all I was left by me father.

MRS. CLEARY [*suddenly*] Nancy, Nancy don't—you might wake Jim before his time.

MRS. HANNIGAN [*replacing umbrella*] I'm ashamed of myself; I never thought about it Mrs. Cleary.

MRS. CLEARY Don't get upset, Miss Tollemache. You didn't know he was in the room at all, and anyway there isn't much wrong with him except him being sleeping like that. I didn't mind once the young doctor made a laugh about what the Aygyptian doctor said. But of course you wouldn't know anything about that Phoebe.

MRS. HANNIGAN [*dryly*] I bet she does.

PHOEBE I know about what the Indian doctor said would happen if he ever recovered his eyesight.

MRS. HANNIGAN We always thought he was an Aygyptian, didn't we Mrs. Cleary? [*acidly*] But of course Miss Tollymachy like the customer is always right.

MRS. CLEARY Well, I did think he was an Aygyptian, too, Miss Tollemache.

PHOEBE No, an Indian. He lived in South—no in North Frederick Street. So the young doctor laughed about it— I hope he's right— but sometimes those Orientals have mysterious ways of penetrating things. [*looking towards bed*] He seems all right, except being a little flushed.

MRS. CLEARY He is all right. To tell the truth, Miss Tollemache, on account of what that ould doctor said, I got a bit of a fright at first thinking he had got some glimmer of the eyesight. But it was a false alarm.

PHOEBE [*looking at* JIM, *musingly*] Yes, I suppose it was. [*going towards door*] Nevertheless I'll feel uneasy about him till he wakes up. You might tell me, Mrs. Cleary.

MRS. CLEARY I will, Miss Tollymache. He won't wake till eight o'clock same as yesterday and the day before. I'll tell you.
[*exit* PHOEBE]

MRS. HANNIGAN Eight o'clock?

MRS. CLEARY I didn't want the poor thing to be coming in again

and worrying herself. By eight o'clock she might have forgotten
about it, and it is better for her to go to bed for herself after being
out all day.

MRS. HANNIGAN You didn't want her to come in worrying you
and your son. That's the truth and you might as well admit it,
Mrs. Cleary. [PHOEBE *is heard playing and singing, 'She is far from
the Land'*] That's a solemn ould thing she's dishin' out this time,
whatever queer notion has come to her.

MRS. CLEARY I recollect she got very solemn when she looked at
him the last time. I wonder could she have spotted anything that
we didn't see.

MRS. HANNIGAN I hope she didn't. Sure there is nothing for her
to spot: isn't he looking in the pink? [*outside someone is heard playing
'The Men of the West' on a whistle*] Here's th' oul whistler now.
The last time I heard him playing that was outside Farrelly's pub
in South King Street, when an unmannerly gent rushed out to him
and asked if he could play cards. He's gone now, I 'spect somebody
hunted him.

MRS. CLEARY I didn't think he was doing it too bad then. Well,
Jim will be waking up very soon now, it's near seven.

MRS. HANNIGAN [*fumbling under jacket*] I never before carried a
watch about with me till I got this affair and it keeps fairly good
time. 'Pon my word, Agnes Cleary, it's gone a quarter past seven
be me ould Ingersoll.

MRS. CLEARY I didn't notice the clock has stopped and you may
be right. 'Tis surprising he isn't waking up. [*goes beside bed and
observes* JIM]

MRS. HANNIGAN He is making some stir now.

MRS. CLEARY He is.

MRS. HANNIGAN Is that a little grunt I hear coming from him?

MRS. CLEARY [*tremulously*] It's some sound, I don't know what it
is. He seems to be in some trouble about something.

MRS. HANNIGAN [*in a husky way*] Trying to wake up maybe and
can't.

MRS. CLEARY [*going rapidly to head of bed*] He's in great trouble.

JIM [*uddenly*] Mother!

MRS. CLEARY [*agonisingly*] Child, child what is it?

JIM [*half-raising himself in bed, loudly and excitedly*] Mother, I see
the moon, I see the moon [*falls back*].

75

MRS. HANNIGAN [*in a shocked way*] He isn't——

MRS. CLEARY He is—he is dead.

MRS. HANNIGAN That oul' Aygyptian was right after all.

MRS. CLEARY He was right.

MRS. HANNIGAN And 'twasn't the moon the poor fella saw either but that ould lamp. It's all the same sure since he thought it was the moon. It gave him a minute of joy anyway, the glame from that ould lamp, and satisfied the wish that was in his mind.

MRS. CLEARY There will be some little consolation to me in that.

MRS. HANNIGAN That parson's daughter is wallopin' away at her ould pianner still. [*goes towards door*] I'll close the door tight so that you won't be hearing her at it.

MRS. CLEARY It is no matter at all. [*outside 'The Men of the West' is heard again*]

MRS. HANNIGAN The whistler is at it again so it's all the same. He's outside the 'Tom Moore' now I'd say or maybe the 'Red Lion'. I'll be back in a minute, and I'll bring Mrs. Durcan and some more of the friends in to be consoling with you and talking to you.

MRS. CLEARY Don't bring anyone to me for a while at any rate. I'd prefer to be alone for a bit.

MRS. HANNIGAN [*hesitatingly and somewhat doubtfully*] It's great you are Agnes Cleary and to take things so cool. It's great, so it is. Well, God bless you my poor woman, anyway.

MRS. CLEARY God bless you also, Nancy Hannigan.

[*exit* MRS. HANNIGAN. *As whistling reaches a crescendo,* MRS. CLEARY *gives a sob and lets head fall on bed*]

CURTAIN

'Twixt The Giltinans and The Carmodys

IN ONE ACT

First printed in THE DUBLIN MAGAZINE New Series Vol XVIII No I
January–March 1943

CHARACTERS

BILLEEN TWOMEY
SHUWAWN DALY, *his aunt*
OLD JANE
MICHAEL CLANCY
BRIDIE GILTINAN
SIMON, *her father*
MAGE, *her mother*
MADGE CARMODY
JAMESIE, *her father*
PEG, *her mother*
FATHER DANSELL

PLACE

Shuwawn Daly's Kitchen

'Twixt The Giltinans and The Carmodys

The scene takes place in the interior of Shuwawn Daly's kitchen. Enter Michael Clancy from front door left. Window by front door. Back door right. Door to adjoining room in back wall.

CLANCY 'Tis all settled now, Shuwawn Daly; and the Giltinans will be here in five minutes. I'm bringing the Giltinan woman first as old Jane there is after telling me the graceful Giltinans have the better of the rogues of Carmodys in Billeen's fancies, this trip.

OLD JANE 'Tis all quiet going. Bridie Giltinan with him for a good bit, Michael Clancy. In troth it could be a month since a word came from him about gamey Madge, and in his fifteen years turn-about court with the pair of them, that's the longest single period I ever seen him stick to either Madge or Bridie.

CLANCY Nevertheless, knowing what Billeen is, and what sudden obstinate flight might not come into that queer old nut of his, I'm bringing the Carmodys as well. But with Tomaus Brack's terrible threat to slaughter him if he isn't married for himself by five o'clock, I have calculated that even if the devil does pinch him to shy at Bridie in the heel, with the short time left to him to save himself, Madge would collar him for a certainty at the rebound.

SHUWAWN Like one greyhound turning the hare, says you, and the other up and nabbing it.

CLANCY For all the world about the same thing, begor, and 'tis well you have said it, Shuwawn Daly. Faith, I had some trouble in arranging the carry-out, giving each family hints that great and final things were about to happen; instructing the Giltinans for their life not to let the Carmodys know a haporth but to steal along for themselves by the boreen, a similar instruction to the Carmodys, but warning them strict to come by the high road and wait behind the ditch till I give them the signal, in a manner they'll never see the Giltinans who'll come in and go out by the front door—the Carmodys coming in by the back, or won't be allowed in at all, of course, according to how the day will go with Bridie. And I have His Reverence planted nice and snug for himself in the little barn waiting to be called as soon as he's wanted.

SHUWAWN The Lord be thankful to you if you can bring Billeen to do the reasonable; and—Glory be to God! Michael Clancy—it's a show, when one comes to ponder over it, to think of that man doting one week on such a girl and the week after, daft about the other—this going on for fifteen years never able to exempt himself from his variations, never able to make up his mind once for all to stick to either the graceful Bridie Giltinan or the gamey Madge Carmody. Bothered I am from watching him and it equal to me which of them he'd take so long as he'd like one or the other, but God grant, whatever, the threat of death in the wind-up will put a diddler to his capers.

CLANCY My confidence he's as good as buckled; still, there's accidents, considering the tortuosity of the likes of him; and 'tis strange to me, Shuwawn, how cool you are sewing away for yourself and your millionaire of a nephew to be slaughtered at five o'clock if it fails him to get spliced. Although it's only a connection of his I am, I'm nearly fit to faint.

SHUWAWN Isn't it my shroud I'm making, Michael Clancy, and Old Jane here, the poor warrant, giving me a hand at it. Besides, it's to reflect the two of us did to-day after you leaving us—the same thought coming into both heads, that there might be some special notion prodding you and you telling us Tomaus Brack was to murder Billeen at five o'clock, we knowing about the arrangement that you were to get two thousand pounds from Billeen as a present the day he was fixed up matrimonial.

CLANCY And if I had another notion—its admitting nothing I am, Shuwawn Daly—but if I had another notion what blame would there be on me, for what good would that two thousand pounds be to me and I dead; then that big debt that's on me and the trouble I have to settle that son of mine on the land. And 'tis yourself was saying Billeen had you bothered, but how happy you would be with your decent living, your nephew in his contentment; and poor Jane there—wouldn't it be an ease to her, likewise, to get the share that's fixed to come to her on his marriage day.

SHUWAWN You are talking, Michael Clancy. My dearest wish

surely is to see Billeen settled down permanently and I do be imagining to myself the pleasure it would be to me to have his youngsters babbling about me, for a bit, whatever, before my latter end.

OLD JANE As for me, Michael Clancy, what I am to get from him never makes no pains for me. But I'd like to have a good feel of the gold that's in his two big trunks. He knows I do be brooding over it and he has promised me the keys to satsify myself the minute he is spliced. My one thought surely, my one wish, to be letting the grand gold and the big white money through my fingers, and hearing the jingle of it and the bing! bing!

CLANCY Isn't it easily she's satisfied, Shuwawn Daly. Still perhaps, 'tis old Jane has the right sense, and in a fair or market day, maybe it's a wiser man I'd be jingling away for myself the few shillings I do be having in the trousers pocket instead of pleasure in my heart thinking of buying porter with it, chatting with the cronies, and sick as a dog the day after. But where's the good in complaining, Shuwawn Daly; temptation is temptation; and without temptation, sez you, what would be left for the priesteens to be doing at all, at all.

SHUWAWN [approvingly] God knows, Michael Clancy, 'tis now you're talking special.

CLANCY However, 'tisn't that is bothering me, but a fear that a thought might come into Billeen's head after, too, like yourselves— that there might be some other notion in the Tomaus Brack threat, and to the two of you I'd be denying no longer it's a make—Tomaus the poor divvle, that hasn't left the bed these three weeks and para- lysed in it, itself. Faith, Billen mightn't be as simple as we think, queer as are his capers about those two girls; making millions in America, he but a common labouring man. Indeed a suspicion sometimes comes to me he could have robbed a share or maybe even murdered a few.

SHUWAWN Lord betune us and harm, Michael Clancy, but 'tis yourself knows he'd never have the spunk to do the like. But we told him the tale about Tomaus as you gave it to us—never men- tioning your name as you ordered. He swallowed it like a crane would swallow a trout; for ever since he was a garsoon when he got a woful massacreeing from that big fellow, and though Billeen is forty years now, the dread of his life is still in him before Tomaus

Brack, and Polyphaymus he always calls him. You can see him below at the bottom of the haggart this minute, shivering and woful.

CLANCY [*giving glance through window, delightedly*] And he is shivering. [*jubilantly*] My plan of campaign is starting gamely, thank God! Getting under way in great style; for all the world like an engine leaving the station, puff! puff! the wheels, moving, a screech and off with it. 'Twas the Muses did it, Shuwawn Daly.

SHUWAWN Or maybe, the Almighty God, Michael Clancy, and it a good thing.

CLANCY The Muses, Shuwawn Daly. Cogitating and pondering I was—'twas yesterday itself and I abroad in our haggard—tormented to the last link with the dint of puzzling was there ere a chance in the world he'd make a right move in the marrying line, no hope of getting a halfpenny out of him till he's married—and a queer turn in him likewise is that obstinate resolve of his. Very well, why, in the middle of my pondering, sir, didn't I stand on a fagot and broke it, and if I did, didn't the rhyme start in the head of me, and sez the rhyme:

> What signify a stick if it does make a crack,
> To fix Rich Billeen, what about Tomaus Brack?

Then the whole notion came—[*noise of latch of back door being risen*] but whist, it's himself—God forbid he should have heard me.

[*enter* BILLEEN, *closing door slowly and looking doubtfully at* MICHAEL, *who is recovering his composure*]

BILLEEN Didn't I know 'twas the sound of a man's voice I was hearing.

CLANCY And the sound of a good man's voice to boot. My blessing on your ears, boy, 'tisn't deaf it has you anyway, whatever is on you and the way you're looking so pale and skeery. A colic maybe, or a touch of that floo?

BILLEEN [*drily*] It could be such and such, Michael Clancy; though it's no common name like that the American doctors would give it; the smartest doctors in the world; and the best of them in Chicago. I got a funny feeling once from taking an overplus of that frish-frash of baked maize and molasses they do be having for the breakfast and a doctor came and cured me but it was something with 'gitis' at the end of it he said I had. If you had only a pain in the big toe its something with 'gitis' at the end of it the Chicago doctor would call it. [*speaking intensely through his teeth and grinning grimly in order to impress*] It's all 'gitis' with them, Michael Clancy.

CLANCY [*as if very interested*] I see. [*suddenly in a tone of levity*] Though from what Shuwawn is after telling me, its hardly a 'gitis' they'd call what will happen to a certain person before five o'clock if his motions and meanderings don't suit one Tomaus Brack, unless it's a 'gitis' they'd say that batch of Cromwell's soldiers got the time the Irish enticed them into a quagmire cut the heads of them like sixty! and the tongues clattering gave the name of Moinveerna to that big bog you have a lovely view of from your hall-door; Moinveerna, Billeen, or if you like it in plain English—the bog of noise.

BILLEEN [*in a shocked way*] The Bog of Noise! But where is the law and the police. What concern is it of Tomaus's when I get married or if I was courting fifty. What right has he to be going on rampageous?

CLANCY [*with a horse-laugh*] What right, says he, talking of murdering-going Tomaus! And faith, 'tisn't like Ulysses he'll escape from this Polyphaymus that isn't trusting to one eye, believe you me, but two of them on him as big as egg-cups and they long in his head like a Chinee. 'Tis in the little slope outside the thing is going to occur, I hear, and alluding to the Cromwellians and the bog, maybe its a new name will be given to Billeen Twomey's pigeon field. Another person told me that all day long since morning Tomaus is sharpening—I nearly imagine I can hear him edging—it could be with that shlane he's going to do it.

BILLEEN [*emitting a horrified little groan, going towards right, rapidly*] It's a bad man you are, Michael Clancy, it's a bad man, for it's gloating over it you are.

CLANCY Faith then, I wisht 'twas myself was in your hobble and the pleasant way you have of getting out of it. She's coming across the yard to us and her father and mother with her. It's Bridie Giltinan I'm alluding to.

BILLEEN [*with a half-silly little smile*] Coming again is it, and she here yesterday. I never seen her so soft and nice and that new pair of Swede shoes she bought in Tralee fitted her grand. A graceful girl is Bridie.

CLANCY Is it sure and certain you are it's her you're fond of then?

BILLEEN I am fond of her.

CLANCY In the name of God then, don't let the time slip on you. There's but an hour left to you to save yourself but 'twill be plenty if the blessing of God is on you, Billeen Twomey.

[*enter* GILTINAN, MRS. GILTINAN *and* BRIDIE *from bakc door, left*]

It's pleased you're looking, Mrs. Giltinan and indeed it's a happy smile is on you, Bridie.

MRS. GILTINAN It's after seeing two magpies we are, Michael Clancy, and don't the old people always say that luck does be following the like, and faix the old people had their own sense, Michael Clancy. God save you, Shuwawn Daly.

SHUWAWN God save you kindly, ma'am. You'll be sitting down now for yourself, Mrs. Giltinan, and you'll all be sitting down.

BILLEEN [*with sudden resolution*] Maybe Bridie might like to come first and see my young gooseberry bush. On the side of the baan I've planted it and it's flourishing fine. I was telling you before about it, Bridie.

BRIDIE [*sweetly*] You were, Billeen. [*modestly, hesitatingly*] But father and mother might like to come with us, Billeen—Mr. Twomey, I mean.

MRS. GILTINAN 'Mr. Twomey', says she, as shy as ever, Billeen. Indeed my darling, and why should we be going with you; it's a long, long time, and so it is, yourself and Billeen are big friends, and I'm thinking it's big friends ye'll be still, when myself and your father, Simon Giltinan, here are cold in our graves for ourselves.

GILTINAN Big friends surely, Mage, they will be; [*meaningly*] and with the help of God maybe it's a good right they will have to be big friends, and, if I spoke it, frightful friends entirely [BILLEEN *and* BRIDIE *go out by door at left of stage*] That wasn't too badly said, was it, Michael Clancy?

CLANCY [*going towards window at left, politely*] What better could it be said, Mr. Giltinan.

MRS. GILTINAN [*in a hushed, eager way*] Is there much of a space between them, Mr. Clancy? I mean are they as close together as what we'd like or expect?

CLANCY [*who has been looking out of window*] They aren't yet, then, in what I would call an exact and suitable state of proximity. [*half to himself, impatiently*] The devil to him—why isn't he? [*more*

84

suavely] They are near the bush now and they are nearer to each other than they were. Ah! the heads are down now and they are whispering.

GILTINAN   Thank God it looks very hopeful.

MRS. GILTINAN   [*piously*] Thank God at last it is.

CLANCY   Here they're back again and faith 'tis quick they're coming. 'Tisn't smiling or blushing she is and there is no happiness in her aspect. [*definitely*] It has failed him. [*suddenly to* GILTINANS] Well, 'tis better for you to be going for yourselves, and I'll argue further with him when you're gone. As I hinted there's a reason why he must marry quick; if he has shied itself, he's fond of your daughter and I think I'll be able to manage him this trip. But strangers would only make Billeen worse when he takes a tie, so in God's name be going and depend on Michael Clancy.

GILTINAN   [*with great earnestness and fine assumption of confidence*] And 'tis on you, sir, we will depend. [*in a loud half-whisper letting* CLANCY *hear*] No harm, Mage, I suppose, if I may mention that beyond in my baan there is a choice grey heifer waiting to be made a present of to someone and what harm would a couple of fivers be along with her?

MRS. GILTINAN   Fifty pounds along with her, Michael Clancy. Well, we'll be going; still, it couldn't be, Michael Clancy, but he made some shape, he all affection and rising the high hopes in us, and 'twill nearly kill me to be off without an agreement come to. [*re-enter* BILLEEN *and* BRIDIE] Oh, Bridie, my darling child isn't it pale you're looking. There's a chill in that east wind my graceful girl. And isn't she graceful, Billeen Twomey, modest and graceful always.

GILTINAN   'Twouldn't describe her, Mage. And though it's of a daughter of my own I'm talking, there isn't a saint under the blue if our Bridie isn't. Gracefulness there is where she is, and virtue there'll be where she'll be.

MRS. GILTINAN   God forbid, Shuwawn Daly, I should be comparing her with that hussy, Madge Carmody, or indeed that I should mention my dutiful family at all in the same breath with that troop. But 'twas yesterday the shame of the world entirely was at the station at their house, when Father Pat who is nice about his feeding—'tisn't like the P.P. who can take what's put before him, he did for his three hard-boiled duck eggs indeed at my own station last week—but Father Pat is different, and not thinking a haporth he just asked my bold Mrs. Carmody to cook him a rasher and egg for his breakfast. 'Yerra', says my trollpe, screeching out before the public, 'cook for you a thing we don't have for ourselves, what a nice thing I'll do', sez she. The people nearly fainted and I was wishing the ground would open and swallow me, Shuwawn Daly.

GILTINAN There's people going—and Shuwawn knows it, Mage—
—that are as you might say, the same as a cow or a horse.

MRS. GILTINAN This morning itself the tally-ho was on by them; and I seen myself that son of theirs, Thade, let fly a bully head of cabbage at his poor old durnawny of a grandfather—out of pure divilment of course. In the kitchen you could hear the father and mother going on and jawning and jawning—I don't know about what. Out in the baan the beauty, Madge was milking that blue cow they call 'Kytie', but the spansel getting loose and the cow kicking the can of milk in Madge, believe you me if my lady didn't let some nice specimens of English out of her. Sure what am I saying?—isn't it more like tinkers than farmers the Carmodys are, and the grace of God isn't about that house, Shuwawn Daly.

GILTINAN The grace of God was never about that house, Mage Giltinan.

MRS. GILTINAN 'Tisn't right to be talking about them at all, Simon, and we'll let them be. But I can't get it from me what has put that change in you, Bridie, if it isn't a chill, a warrant would think it was downhearted you were, maybe after having a little quarrel with your old friend, though I couldn't believe now it would be anything cross or queer Billeen said to you.

BRIDIE [*brokenly*] Is it Billeen, mother, say anything cross! and indeed [*meaningly*] it's nothing anyway did he say, mother dear.

BILLEEN [*who has gone to dresser and during foregoing dialogue was giving painful if silent evidence of his uneasiness whilst all the time pinching the top of his boot with a stick*] But I'm going to write it. I'm going to write what I wanted to say, Mrs. Giltinan. It's after telling Bridie I am. I mean, Mrs. Giltinan, there was some little thing I wanted to say to Bridie at the bush, only someway I couldn't but the minute I'm in my lonesome I'm going to write to and send it over, Mrs. Giltinan.

BRIDIE [*drearily*] Yes, mother, he said he was going to write it.

CLANCY [*aside to* GILTINAN *and* MRS. GILTINAN] Then let him write it. And the quicker you'll go the quicker 'twill be done.

GILTINAN   In the name of God then, Mage, off with us.

MRS GILTINAN   And we are off [*aside to* MICHAEL] A hundred pounds going with that heifer, Michael Clancy. Be putting on your shawl and be coming Bridie, my darling. We'll be on tip-toe for the note from Mr. Twomey, and a nice graceful reply she will give to it, Billeen.

[GILTINANS *go out by left door*]

CLANCY [*going quickly to* BILLEEN] You scabbafluter, no denying it in me now—it's the way it's Madge with you again.

BILLEEN   I couldn't deny it in you, Michael. For three days something inside in my mind was urging me back once more in her preference, but I didn't know it rightly till it was coming to the points with me and Bridie.

CLANCY [*going to door at right and beckoning to* CARMODYS, *unperceived*] Madge is the girl in the heel, then, and you are thoroughly sure of yourself with the moments shortening for your life's salvation?

BILLEEN [*beating top of boot with stick, leering half-idiotically*] It's all Madge with me, and I am thoroughly sure of myself; [*musingly*] She is gay; [*with some excitement*] Madge is terrible gay; [*very excitedly and enthusiastically*] She's as gay as the divil itself, Michael Clancy.

CLANCY   You are the lucky man, then, and she walking in to you. Or maybe it's your prayers you said this morning, and 'tis the will of God is sending the Carmody's to you in the nick of time.

[*enter* CARMODY, MRS. CARMODY *and* MADGE *by back door at right*]

CARMODY [*jovially*] Oh, it's fine to be young and be married; it's fine to be courting all day. No harm in being jolly in oneself, Shuwawn Daly.

SHUWAWN   Far from it, Mr. Carmody.

CARMODY   And though you mightn't believe it, Shuwawn, but it's God's truth, long as we're coupled at all, 'tis an occasional court myself and the old woman do be having still [*catching* MRS. CARMODY] And, what about a rowl now, Peg, you funny thing.

MRS. CARMODY [*laughing and dashing away from him*] Will you behave you shameless old beardy puss, or what will that decent, modest, illigant 'by' Billeen Twomey, think of us, at all, at all. But no harm in Jamesie, Billeen, only his capers.

CARMODY [*cheerily to* MICHAEL] My woman is a fine woman, Michael Clancy. My bluebell I call her, but sometimes I calls her my ox-eyed daisy.

SHUWAWN Ye'll be sitting down now, and be settling the forum, Jane.

BILLEEN [*edging towards door at left*] If Madge wouldn't like to come first and see the new black-currant tree I have planted. Would you be coming, Madge?

MADGE Faix I will and hopping [*as* BILLEEN *appears a little irresolute*] Why wouldn't I, Billeen.

BILLEEN [*slyly*] Only wondering I was if it isn't the father and mother you'd be wishing escorting us.

MADGE [*in a scream*] The pa and ma, is it! That I mightn't sin now, but who would expect it from Billeen Twomey to be starting the like of that for a joke. The da and ma [*laughing loudly*] Well, glory be to God, Billeen!

BILLEEN [*laughing similarly and looking up to her gayly*] Well glory be to God, Madge.

[*they go out front door, left, rapidly emitting spurts of laughter*]

CARMODY [*triumphantly*] By this and by that, in the finish 'tis Madge has him nabbed. And, we not even half hoping for it, itself. Why aren't you lepping, Peg?

MRS. CARMODY Isn't it lepping out of the skin I am, and what blame would you have on me, Shuwawn Daly.

CARMODY Is he ketching her, Michael Clancy? He is, of course, and don't be telling me he isn't.

CLANCY [*looking out of window*] Faith they're as gay as bees for themselves, talking and trotting making for the bush. It looks as good as settled. Whist! she has made a slip letting on to be falling giving him the chance to put the arm around her. He didn't and she didn't fall no less, but hesht! they're at the bush. They are close to one another, they are desperate close to one another—they're clapped up to one another—oh—they're—

CARMODY [*excitedly*] Embracing and kissing and canoodling and fondling.

MRS. CARMODY [*ditto*] Embracing and kissing and canoodling and fondling.

CLANCY [*grimly*] God knows they *are* not, but back again with them. [*savagely*] Well, glory to all that's good! She's making a shape at laughing surely, but faith, I can see she's no longer gay. Bad luck to him! or is it the devil himself has made him shy this trip.

CARMODY Begob, he mustn't shy, we sure of him and she sure of him. He must have decency or may be there might be a way to force him.

MRS. CARMODY If there could be a way!

CLANCY Better leave him alone to me for a bit—depend on me to do the necessary.

MRS. CARMODY Do as the man says, Jamesie, Michael Clancy is our friend.

CARMODY And as he says, I will do, Peg; still, Michael wouldn't be blaming me to make some scrape, and it looking such a certainty and it was a certainty. [*re-enter* BILLEEN *and* MADGE] 'Tis my gay girl, Madge, again, is it? Though indeed it was a deal gayer I was expecting you to be returning, and as gleeful as you went out my charmer.

MADGE [*drily*] Sure it's gay enough I am; [*with some asperity*] and likewise is Billeen. But it's under the poplars he'll be twice as gay, he says. For it's going to ride the horse over to our house he is, and its under the poplar he's going to say something important to me, for it's more romantic under the poplar, he says.

BILLEEN [*desperately*] You see it's something romantic I was thinking of saying to Madge, Mr. Carmody, and it's under the poplar I would like to say it. In two minutes I'll be on the horse and over, and it won't take me two minutes itself.

CARMODY [*somewhat menacingly*] And under the poplar she will be fine; but, though it's her father says it—it's fine she'd be and fine enough for that man that ever lived if it's under a common gosedaun he found her itself, Billeen Twomey. Who in the parish can sew and knit and bake the best? Madge Carmody. Who the topper at milking a cow or feeding a calf or a pig?—Madge Carmody. Who the cleverest, stylishest farmer's daughter walking down to Mass? Madge Carmody. Who makes the butter sells best in the market and who has the hens lays all the eggs?—Madge Carmody. Maybe she hasn't spunk. But all the world knows of the day the police and bailiffs were ready to make that dart to sweep Dan Curtin's farm, and going to the stable what did they find?—the horses were there but the harness was gone. I won't say who did it—maybe 'twas a man did it—it could be still if I was asked plain and straight maybe I would answer or maybe I would answer—Madge Carmody.

MRS. CARMODY [*clinching the matter*] And it was Madge Carmody.

CARMODY How now about dowdy eyes-in-the-mire, Bridie Giltinan. How now about all the Giltinans, sneaking hypocrites, father, mother, daughter and every mother's soul of them inside in that shanty of theirs. Their letting on to be devout and their capers about being extra select in themselves—'twould sicken a pig. 'Tisn't alluding to you I am, Billeen, but that same Bridie would marry an oldish man for his cash and make a cuckhold of him, like Maureen-so-fine and her poor old anghashore of a husband with his 'gwan agin' to the ass driving her into town and she sitting up in the seat of the car sticking out the tongue at him behind his back and making fun for the passers.

MRS. CARMODY God knows then, she used so, Jamesie. She used, Billeen.

CARMODY Billeen himself knows about it and how Maureen used be clinking glasses in Tivy's public house making a pure fool of the pure old hubby and she giving him the toast—'here's to you, my dear', was how she had it—'and not to you my dear, for if he was here that should be here 'tisn't to you I'd drink, my dear', the gom thinking she was acting, till she went off with a tinker leaving him a pauper. The same sly go was on Maureen before she married that's now on sleekly slimy Bridie Giltinan.

MRS CARMODY The dead spit of one another; Jamesie is telling the truth, Billeen.

CARMODY But it's after marrying that the divvil does be always pinching them sly-gowers—the wrong time—whereas with likes of fine open, jolly Madge and their innocent frolics—once they're spliced they are spliced and *aus go bragh* with capers.

BILLEEN [*in an agonized way*] I'll be on the horse in one minute, Mr. Carmody; if I'll get the minute.

CLANCY [*to* CARMODY] Telling you again I am, depend on me.

MRS. CARMODY Be said by Mr. Clancy. [*to* MICHAEL] And no harm meant if I was saying to you that another hundred pounds or so would be as good in your pocker as in that of the next, along with what will be coming to you from the millionaire.

CARMODY Two hundred—three hundred—four hundred, 'tis generous people we are whatever the Giltinans might be, and I'll go farther and say Michael Clancy, what's ours is yours. We will depend on you. Come, Madge, my gago, [*with forced cheeriness*] and I'll bet a shilling Billeen will be first at the poplar.

[CARMODYS *go out back door right*]

BILLEEN Don't be blaming me too much, Michael. I was surely fixed and we at the bush, but for Madge's own fault to let fall the remark about the Missioners coming next week. Then the picture of Bridie rose up before me, and, glory be to God! as plain as I could see her in the middle of the chapel, all devotion, her two eyes in one gaze on the prayching Missioner on the altar. It put the kybosh complete on what I was going to say to Madge; though I like Madge, but in the wind-up I don't know what way I am.

CLANCY [*grimly*] 'Twill be equal to you in a quarter of an hour's time which is which; though Bridie will still be Bridie and Madge will still be Madge.

BILLEEN [*woefully*] Let me think and let me try; let me think, Michael Clancy.

CLANCY What time is there for thinking and trying, fooleen? [*vigorously*] Out with it and let it be said: is it that writin' pin I'll get for you or will you mount that horse?

BILLEEN The horse. Oh, give me the pin! No, it's the horse I want. No—it's the pin I want—or is it?

CLANCY [*losing all patience*] The horse or the pin; the pin or the horse; the horse or the pin, the pin or the horse.

BILLEEN [*blankly*] The horse or the pin, the pin or the horse. My God, if I can decide, death facing me and all! Pray for me, Shuwawn pray for me, Old Jane! The horse or the pin—the pin—

[*re-enter, rushing,* CARMODYS *and* GILTINANS *by back door*]

GILTINANS *and* CARMODYS [*all shouting*] They thought we wouldn't meet, but we did meet. And fifteen years he's at it, a labouring man that was to be making a joke and a jeer of decent farmers' daughters. All together at him; there's six of us in it, but there'll be a bit of him for each of the six.

CLANCY Will you let me say one word itself?

BILLEEN [*stricken with fright*] Be merciful and be listening to Michael; he'll explain, I'm telling you, he will.

GILTINANS *and* CARMODYS And you'll explain—but maybe 'tis in Heaven you'll make the explanation. But give a talking to him, girls, first.

BRIDIE Indeed, Billeen, how can you ever get over or explain the humbug you have made of me or the wrong you have done me in the heel. But sure, I needn't be upbraiding you singly, haven't you been doing the same to her as to a poor innocent creature like me.

MADGE [*who had come opposite* BRIDIE] Listen to that—alluding to me insulting as 'her' and I as innocent as herself? And it's soft you're speaking to him, and a minute ago we all fixed how to give it to him. 'Tis a traitor you have turned in a hop thinking to capture him by a mean shift and you still having hopes of Billeen.

MRS. GILTINAN [*sweetly, to* MRS. CARMODY] Indeed, there was no harm now in what Bridie said and she meaning nothing by it, Mrs. Carmody.

MRS. CARMODY What pratin' so, had she of her innocence? 'Tis curious and so it is, Mrs. Giltinan.

MRS. GILTINAN [*sweetly as before*] Now don't the world know, Mrs. Carmody, that there is a certain little difference between Bridie and Madge, but this isn't the time to be arguing about it, and we won't be arguing about it.

CARMODY [*loudly*] What difference is the woman talking about? Champion to you, Madge, and I'd like to see who's going to act the tony forninst you.

MADGE So would I, father dear. And, Miss Bridie Giltinan, don't dare allude to me again as 'her', I'm warning you.

BRIDIE A threatening look in her bad eye, mother, the wickedness breaking out in her. Didn't Father Debbing say honest people had the right to defend themselves against those that would do them harm, and though I'm innocent, it's no fool I am, Madgie, and you won't gain points by having the first go whatever, this trip. [*makes a dart and catches* MADGE *by hair*]

MRS. GILTINAN The Grace of God be our shield, darling, and I'm not going to be massacred first no less if I can help it.
[*grabs hold of* MRS. CARMODY]

CARMODY [*making for* GILTINAN] Another treacherous hypocrite thinking to be first here; but faith you won't all be first.
[*catches hold of* GILTINAN]

GILTINAN A blackguard Carmody wishing to down me—but you

haven't me downed yet. Don't be giving the leg you hound of a devil itself.

CARMODY You sneaking crawler, 'tis you is giving the leg. Leave off your kicking or I'll stamp you into dust, I'm telling you.

MADGE [*who has been struggling fiercely with* BRIDIE] I'll pick the eyes out of your head and I'll bite.

BRIDIE You will if you get a vacancy; but I have you by the hair and I won't leave a nose or an ear on you.

MRS. CARMODY [*who has been making vigorous efforts to free herself from* MRS. GILTINAN'S *grasp, suddenly, screaming*] She has me by the throat, the murderess! Jamsie, Jamsie, she's choking me!

CLANCY [*suddenly*] It's some say I must have, and I order it—out with the whole lot of you that has been a torment to this place for fifteen years, but a fitter thing it would have been to have looked out for common husbands for your common daughters than chasing a millionaire; and, if I wanted it fixed up with one or either in the finish, 'twas through compassion for this poor bothered woman, Shuwawn Daly. As a near connection of same, it's my right to ask the man of the house, the man of the house himself being in a state of *non compus mentis* and again I'm telling you to clear out of it if you don't want the temper to rise and you know what it is when it does rise—the temper of Michael Clancy. [*short pause*] You aren't going? Very well, why? The temper has risen, and now it's your blood I want, and it's your blood I will have, and it's your blood I must have.

[*goes to back wall, takes four-prong pike and faces* GILTINANS *and* CARMODYS]

BILLEEN [*in a panic, rushing out back-door*] O! Glory! But don't kill'em all, Michael Clancy, don't kill'em all!

[*as* BILLEEN *goes out back door,* CLANCY *at pike-point forces* GILTINANS *and* CARMODYS *out by front. He closes door, turns around*]

CLANCY [*shouting to* BILLEEN] Come in again! [BILLEEN *re-enters cautiously*] Only six minutes left to you to live. That was why I was in such a hurry out with the Giltinans and the Carmodys, letting on to be vexed, but a new thought having come to me and I seeing you were done forever with both gangs, and either of those girls being unsuitable for you anyway. The Muses again, Shuwawn Daly, in a manner it must be a real poet I'm becoming in the heel of my days, and a real poet could stick his fingers in a cow-dung and verify his immortality in a cow-horn for you; 'tisn't like the sham poets settling themselves at a table, fixing the papers in front of them as nice as nicety, knocking a drop of ink off the pen on the floor, gauging and shaping, like a sergeant peeler making out a report gloating over his caligraphy, or a National Taycher concocting a figario for the Inspector. I admit the inspiration came to me through those lines of sham-poet O'Rourke and he telling us:

> Happy we should be sez he we're not roasting in Hell,
> Or that dogs can't talk, or that people can't smell.

The lines were running in my head and the Muses began working me through one word, 'people'. So the rhyme came to me and sez the rhyme:

> The people can be laughing and the rain can go to Spain,
> But the woman for Billeen is our darling old Jane.

BILLEEN [*taken aback, coming towards front of stage, cautiously*] Old Jane is it?

CLANCY Old Jane it is. Not alone will she be the means of saving your life, but who has the best right to you than the dacent girl that's slaving for your Aunt all her days and for you to boot since you came back from Chicago. Long ago I would have thought of it and she matching you down to the ground but for the way you were meandering between the pair of lassies, Besides, Old Jane is only a nickname and she wanting three years to the age is on you, Billeen.

BILLEEN [*decidedly*] God knows, she is not, but is three years older than me, Michael Clancy.

CLANCY Her sister, Martha, you're thinking of that was six years your elder and is dead for twenty. Shuwawn can back me up and she knowing the age of both of them.

SHUWAWN [*judiciously*] I'd rather leave it to yourself, Michael Clancy. It's queer entirely the memory is by me, and 'tis Thomas Clobber itself made out my own age for me and I looking for the pinsion. Billeen will take your word for it, and in all the matter why wouldn't he be said by you.

94

CLANCY He will, and let us consider the match made. A whistle will bring Father Dansell.

BILLEEN Oh bierna! to be married by a suspended priest to boot.

CLANCY Whist! isn't he taken back again, and if he isn't itself, they will have as much virtue the words he will say over you as if they were pronounced by His Eminence himself. [*priest enters quietly by front door*] Oh, it's yourself that's in it, Father.

PRIEST Isn't it long waiting I was, and 'tis dozing I was when I was hearing noises, noises, and wondering I was, and shivering with the cold I was from waiting itself.

CLANCY The fault the gamey bridegroom's your reverence. But you have come in on the tip and now it's ready and impatient he is.

BILLEEN [*shaking head*] It's suspecting something I am.

CLANCY [*coming to* BILLEEN, *aside to latter*] Suspecting the decent priest, is it, and the crature after putting himself in danger of catching the flu waiting to do you a good turn and he knowing about Tomaus. Here, be settling yourself in a position before his reverence.

BILLEEN [*going near window, with sudden resolution, sharply*] I will not, Michael Clancy; I will not again, I'm saying.

CLANCY [*pointing at window, in hollow tones*] Will you have time, anyway, and Tomaus moving southwards. The big black head of him is above the brow of that little hill, now.

BILLEEN A reek of turf a head? Finuicane's reek and I know it.

CLANCY [*evenly*] The hearse plumes shaking—the hearse-plumes Tomaus dons when the blood-lust is maddening him. Deluded and blinded you are for faith 'tisn't the like of them would be shaking on a reek of turf, my poor man.

BILLEEN [*overwhelmed with terror*] Plumes and not rushes! The murderer, 'tis him! I don't want to be slaughtered and I'm ready, Michael Clancy [*goes before* PRIEST]

PRIEST The man is here but the woman is making no shift. [*sharply*] How is that, Mr. Clancy? Isn't it agreeable, she is?

CLANCY [*going quietly to* OLD JANE] My doing, your reverence. It's waxing a coord to splice a bail-rod I was, with my awkwardness didn't I leave the ball of wax on the seat. [*pulling* JANE *up*] It's loosened she is your reverence [*shoving her forcibly on to beside* BILLEEN] She'd nearly have run into your reverence but I stopping her, it's a wild wan entirely she is, your reverence.

95

8

PRIEST [*to* BILLEEN] Will you have this woman to be your lawful wedded wife?

BILLEEN I won't. [*correcting himself quickly*] I will, I mean.

PRIEST [*to* JANE] Will you have this man to be your lawful wedded husband?

OLD JANE [*stolidly*] I ought, I suppose, and I should.

PRIEST [*stormily*] Woman! it's assisting at the Sacrament of Marriage you are, and 'tisn't the way you can surely be as ignorant that you don't know how to answer a silly thing.

OLD JANE Faith, what could I know about it, your reverence, that never expected to go through the like, a single woman since the day I was borned and never thinking of nothing at all, at all.

PRIEST Again I'm asking you, will you have this man to be your lawfully wedded husband?

CLANCY [*intensely, in* OLD JANE'S *ear*] Is it wishing you are to have me dead right on the spot? Say 'I will', you divil!

OLD JANE Very well, sure. [*to* PRIEST] I will, then.

[PRIEST *concludes ceremony*]

BILLEEN [*to* MICHAEL, *pulling note from pocket*] There's but a ten pound note in the pocket, and it's ashamed I am to offer as little to His Reverence.

CLANCY [*taking note and handing it to priest*] 'Tis little surely, but wait till you start making up your accounts, and your reverence needn't be surprised if an envelope comes to you to-morrow with a cheque for fifty thousand in it and Billeen a millionaire.

PRIEST [*taking note*] Indeed, it's a long time since I had the feel of a ten-pound note in my fist; and 'tisn't wild wishes I'll let into my mind because of your funny talk of fifty thousand, or get into a state like some that buys tickets for huge sweepstake, their brains heating with the puzzle of what they would do with the big money when they'd win it, troubled over it, making themselves unhappy about it, and their chance of coming by it about the same as that of their being able to reach the North Star. Futility! Futility! No, I won't be dreaming about the fifty thousand, Mr. Clancy, but this ten-pound note is in my fist and being in my fist it is a fact. I can buy a new pair of boots with it and I can buy—[*with a curious little smile*] —Well, God bless you all. [*goes out*]

BILLEEN 'Tis queer the way they do be expressing themselves for suspended priests. Indeed 'twas the queer marrying altogether, no right ring, no nothing, but he taking a tin ring and putting it on Jane—a bit touched surely—but God help me—'tisn't impudent a warrant could be to a priest. What will the big Twomey's think of me, my big relations of farmers, and I having it planned to have the grand marriage entirely, to take the shine out of them, I that was once a poor boy? 'Tis miserable it is.

CLANCY [*coming from front door*] Whist! it's now in your safety you are and the priest after meeting with Thomaus Brack. What hindrance will there be to a rich man like you having another marriage in the chapel to-morrow for yourself with carriages and soppers and all.

OLD JANE [*going to* BILLEEN, *vacantly*] Rings and marriage, rings and marriages! But [*intensely*] your promise to me—and the keys, Billeen, the keys!

[BILLEEN *takes bunch of keys from pocket and hands them to her; she goes rapidly towards room, vainly endeavouring to conceal the signs of her avidity from* MICHAEL, *who, she knows, is intently watching her. She goes into room leaving door partly ajar. A rattle of locks being opened is heard and a loud clink of coins. Shortly, the noise of the coins becomes more regular*]

CLANCY [*bending himself forward*] She's counting, Shuwawn Daly.

SHUWAWN [*extending her head in direction of open door*] She is counting.

CLANCY I can see through the slit between the jamb and the door. Standing she is, and faith 'tis strange, but 'tis sour enough the puss is on her.

BILLEEN [*as if a sudden revelation had come to him*] The dots and the nought-noughts!

CLANCY [*turning to* BILLEEN] Eh?

[OLD JANE *comes dwon from room and goes to* BILLEEN]

OLD JANE Here's your money, and here's your keys, Billeen. And 'tis all the money and all the millions—and all the millions is but three hundred and twenty pounds, Michael Clancy. There's a hundred and twenty on deposit receipt, and eight in bank notes; and the millions in gold is but a few sovereigns and half sovereigns, half-crowns and florins, sixpenny bits and threepenny bits and fourpenny bits, a couple of bob and some coppers, making up the balance—a matter of twenty pounds, Michael Clancy.

[*goes to seat, sits down. Looks entirely unhappy*]

CLANCY [*in a tone of hollow anger and forced scepticism*] Apish you're talking, woman, in the last stage of your ignorance.

OLD JANE Maybe; but if it's no hand I was able to make of the parsing and geography itself the time I was going to school, it's noted I was for Algebra and the Arithmetic in a manner Mrs. Mahanny, the taycher, used say I'd do great inside the counter; and Jug Doolan and Ned Oge and my sister Martha—God rest their souls! they're all dead now—they used to be saying it's the topper all out I'd have made of an egg-merchant. And Billeen's fortune not counting the halfpence and farthings is three hundred and twenty pounds to a tick, Michael Clancy.

BILLEEN 'Twas the dots and the nought-noughts in the dotted bills did it, and when I took out that deposit receipt for a heap of them the time I came back, everyone saying 'twas a million I was after putting in the Bank, yourself saying it as well as the next, Michael Clancy, didn't I come to believe it was a million and that I was ninety-nine times richer than I thought I was not having rightly comprehended as I imagined the value and the meaning of the dots and the nought-noughts.

CLANCY [*dully, savagely*] The dots and the nought-noughts!

BILLEEN [*in reminiscent fashion*] And anyway—and I don't know why—I was never able to bring myself to look at that deposit receipt. But I now recall that my cousin, Michael Foran, that keeps a dry goods store in West 49th Street—199B is the number of his house, Michael Clancy—he did say to me surely and I leaving Chicago: 'there's £1,850 in the wallet by you', said he, 'and be careful of it', said he.

CLANCY Only £1,850! But if you had that much now itself or even the half of it, you might be able to give some help to the friends. For the four cows and the bit of land you bought you only paid £550 all told: 'tis the same clothes you're wearing you brought back from America, and a farthing you never gave to your own; whilst out of the little all you ever had there is over a thousand pounds gone to Hong Kong between the Giltinans and the Carmodys, with every fair day, market day or sports day would rise over you in Abbeyfeale, Duagh or Listowel, 'twould be the case with you of sweets or things for Bridie or pies of fal-als for Madge. Faith, it wasn't queer the priest was expressing himself, a solid ten quid in his pocket and nothing in Michael Clancy's but futility [*with sudden wildness taking off his hat and turning towards* SHUWAWN], Anamon dhoul it's mad I'm going entirely. [*bending*] It's a good stroke is in that long bony arm by you still, Shuwawn Daly, and take this stick and smash this skull and knock what's in it out of it, for the brains that are in that head have no right to be in the head of Michael Clancy.

BILLEEN [*excitedly*] It's rightly cracked you are, and the woman up to the age for doting. In the name of God don't think, of it, Shuwawn. And I won't leave you minus entirely Michael Clancy [*going to* MICHAEL] And I'm thinking there's just a hundred in this bundle of notes (*hands bundle to* MICHAEL *who becomes suddenly mollified*] Poh! why wouldn't I? We'll be well enough off with over two hundred and twenty and our bit of a farm and our four cows, and Shuwawn has her pension. Anyway, 'tisn't the loss of the millions, but the queer marrying is troubling me most at the present moment.

CLANCY [*counting in a satisfied way*] Tin and tin make twenty and tin makes thirty—thirty-five—forty—

OLD JANE [*grimly*] What concern is a queer marrying and what concern is deposit receipts. But was there ever known the likes of my disappointment and never will I have what I thought I'd have —the feel of the grand gold. Fifteen years dreaming over it—the big pieces of the yellow gold, the golden guineas and the gold dollars thick and a great weight on them, and the fine white money; they going through my fingers and I taking them up in fistful and fistful [*almost blubbering*]; the jingly, Michael Clancy, and the bing! bing!

MICHAEL [*finishing counting*] Tin makes a hundred. [*puts bundle into side pocket with an air of content and satisfaction*] Well no good in lamenting now, anyway, Old Jane, and Billeen needn't be having his worry no less, and the pair of ye married enough.

BILLEEN Married, but not as could properly be said—celebrated. That's what they always say in Chicago when people are rightly married—they say the marriage was celebrated, Michael Clancy.

CLANCY Well now, that is smart talk, Billeen; for in the very last number of the 'Kerry Star', the paper did refer to a marriage between two respectables as having been celebrated—upon my soul it did.

BILLEEN [*sententiously, with an air of superiority*] If it did itself, it's

99

from Chicago it got it, Michael Clancy. But it's alluding I am, since the priest didn't do the suitable in the line of celebrating, couldn't we make some shift to give an air of celebration to the marrying ourselves? We can buy a ring to-morrow, bit in other respects we might make some little shapes [*to* OLD JANE] Anyway, will we kiss? [SHUWAWN *and* MICHAEL *nod approvingly*]

OLD JANE [*observing nod, rising as it were unwillingly, with dreary intonation*] If so be, then, sure I suppose we might as well.

[OLD JANE *and* BILLEEN *move slowly towards one another, showing signs of antagonism rather than affection. They embrace grimly and determinedly, and a loud kiss is heard.*]

CURTAIN

The Simple Hanrahans

IN THREE ACTS

Here first printed from the manuscript

CHARACTERS

MICHAEL HANRAHAN, *farmer, old*
MRS. HANRAHAN, *his wife*
LENA, *their daughter*
MAURICE, *his brother*
THEOBALD MUNNIX, *farmer, middle-aged*
MRS. MUNNIX, *his wife*
PETE, *their son*
EILEEN, *their daughter*
DAISY, *a bar-maid*
BILLY ROCHE, *a process-server*
JAYMARY GUNN, *National Teacher*

PLACE

A public-house bar (Act I); the Munnix's kitchen (Act II); the Hanrahan's kitchen (Act III).

TIME

Approximately the same as the duration of the stage presentation.

The Simple Hanrahans

ACT I

The scene takes place in a public-house bar in a small town. At extreme left, entrance door from street; to right of this, little door of 'snug'; at extreme right are shelves well-stocked with bottles of whiskey, wines, etc. The shelves behind bar-counter also have bottles of liquor, as well as a varied assortment of wares such as jams, biscuits, sweets, corn-cures, aspirins, etc. Behind the counter, seated on a high stool, is Daisy the bar-maid reading, or pretending to read a newspaper

Enter, jauntily, BILLY ROCHE *and* JAYMARY GUNN

ROCHE How-dee-do, Daisy? Not a stir, just a nod.

GUNN And a curt one. However, give us two halves of Redbreast, miss, if you please.

ROCHE It's out of pride she's going on. I forgot this was Tuesday which is Daisy's proud day, when she won't serve drinks herself but rings for her ma.

DAISY [*indifferently*] You don't say!

ROCHE You needn't be so top-lofty even if this is your ma's pub, since by virtue of your stactus.

GUNN Status.

ROCHE Of your status veesta-veest—

GUNN Vis-a-vis.

ROCHE Veezy-vee of the customers you're only a barmaid which, my daughter tells me, who does crosswords, is nicknamed a big ale over in England.

GUNN [*lightly*] Don't get riled, Miss Farrelly. A misconception on my friend's part—not three words but one—A.B.I.G.A.I.L. Abigail a biblical character.

DAISY [*putting paper aside and preparing to get off stool, sententiously*] Oh, thank you, Mr. Gunn. [*she gets off stool*]

ROCHE [*brusquely*] What about them two halves of Redbreast?

103

DAISY *[pertly]* I'm not deaf. So, who said which and who said what.

ROCHE *[nudging* GUNN*]* Look taycher, see how she's passed the sealed bottle, and gone to the one with th'ould cork in it—as sure as my life the bottle her ma put the water in.

DAISY *[pours whiskey into glasses. firmly]* My mother never does no such a thing! A woman who goes to her devotions every day of the week to do the like! Except, of course—

ROCHE *[sardonically]* Except what?

DAISY *[scornfully]* If you don't understand your intelligent friend the taycher will that if a business is not run on business-like lines, bankruptcy is inscrutable—I mean indelible—in—in—in—

GUNN Inevitable, I'd say, perhaps.

DAISY Inevitable, yes, and if we didn't make up for the breakage of glasses, where would we be? To charge for them is against custom, so to penalise matters—

GUNN Or to equalise them?

DAISY To equalise matters, my mother might put a small sup of water in a bottle occasionally. Of course, she only gives that whiskey to certain people.

ROCHE *[with a loud horse-laugh]* To the people who break the glasses, is it?

GUNN *[gaily]* Now, Bill, we must really compliment Daisy on her charming candour, and we are constrained to admit that there are two sides to every question—our opinion on one side of the counter and Miss Daisy's view on hers—*n'est ce pas?*

ROCHE I don't know anything about her pa. It's her ma I'm referring to.

DAISY My mother you mean?

ROCHE Your ma I said.

DAISY Like a child.

ROCHE Well, I have the heart of a child. The very words by the way your competitor up the street, Mrs. Quirke, another devout woman like your ma, used, when at last she was hauled up for watering the whiskey, doing it for years and making a fortune out of it. That's what she said that she was like a child, that it wasn't for money she was doing it at all but for the good of people's souls and that a drunken man was never seen to leave her house, so that the Justice who was a fanatical taytotaller congratulated her on her high calculation to—on her loftly dilutions to—

GUNN   On her high devotion to lofty ideals.

ROCHE   Exactly what he said and instead of fining her, wrote a letter
to the headquarters of the tay total Association in Dublin who
presented her with a medal.

DAISY   [*with utter incredulity, screaming with laughter*] You're telling
me!

ROCHE   Don't be doubting me, I couldn't say the Judge was a rogue
or a fool for if I did in these days, I might be convicted of lazy
magesty.

GUNN   You might be convicted of *lese majeste*, if you referred in such
opprobrious terms to a Departmental inspector not to mind a
Judge. Be careful, Billeen, of your apostrofication of our uncrowned
kings.

DAISY   [*slyly*] I thought it was only the Inspector of National Schools
was such a big fellow as that.

GUNN   Oh, he's better, he's an emperor. [*promptly*] In fact, he's
worse—a damn sight worse—he's the Grand Cham of Tartary.

ROCHE   [*interrupting*] For heaven's sake, Daisy, give us two more
Redbreasts.

GUNN   [*jocosely*] I shudder when I think of the Grand Cham [*to
ROCHE*], but why should you look worried? Thinking perhaps that
the tie you are wearing appears to Daisy to be a bit too swanky for a
process-server. She looks sententious. All barmaids have conser-
vative minds.

ROCHE   I misdoubt it's the tie that's pinching her.

GUNN   [*as DAISY serves drinks*] Thanks beauty—thanks awfully.

ROCHE   Come Daisy, out with it. I don't believe it's this ould two-
and-sixpenny tie is the cause of you giving me underlooks. You
know we are going to the wedding of Pete Munnix and Lena
Hanrahan, and maybe it's your notion that because I hold the rather
unexalted position of a process-server that I'm not a suitable person
to attend such a festivity.

DAISY   [*gaily*] Go on wid yez! I'd like to know who'd call you a
process-server to your face except your chum the taycher here, and
whenever you go out on your biz, leaving big empty blue envelopes
on the fields after you with Civil Bill Officer printed on them and
you puffed up with pride showing the swanky job you have got.

GUNN   [*amusedly*] She has you there, Billeen, I picked up one or two
of those empty envelopes myself but probably due to a form of

congenital obtuseness on my part I failed to comprehend the subtle implication of your blue residualities.

ROCHE   Well, as you would say yourself taycher, out of the wells—out of the deeps—

GUNN   Out of the depths.

ROCHE   Out of the depths of your verbosity, it's an allowable weakness anyway considering the respectable yeoman farmer I originally sprang from, but owing to the thingum a jig of circs.—the exilarie of existence and the figgilness of—of—

GUNN   The exigencies of existence and the fickleness of fortune—

ROCHE   I was driven holeus—boleus [*short pause*] it isn't holeus-boleus—

GUNN   Nolens-volens—

ROCHE   To achieve—to accept such a mangy possession.

GUNN   [*smilingly*] To adopt such a mangy profession.

DAISY   [*laughing*] The both of yez get on well together [*slyly*] and I have heard how you collaborated in another little matter. It's no wonder you'd be jolly in yourselves going to Pete Munnix's wedding.

ROCHE   [*aside to* GUNN] Didn't I know she had something up her sleeve. [*suddenly, brusquely to* DAISY] What are you hinting at now?

GUNN   [*reprovingly*] Please don't address a young lady with such indiplomatic and untactful directness. [*smoothly*] Mademoiselle, may we humbly inquire what may be the mysterious import of you circumlocutory exordium?

ROCHE   I can guess it. It's about that five acre green field of mine the simple Hanrahans walked into—the gate being open—the day they were matchmaking with the Munnixes, thinking it belonged to the said Munnixes, not knowing I had a right-of-way through the Munnixs' land.

GUNN   [*laughing*] Ha! ha! ha!

ROCHE   [*ditto*] Ha! ha! ha! Surely 'tisn't going to strangers like the Hanrahans I'd be and informing against a next door neighbour, thereby reducing the amount of fortune Lena Hanrahan would bring to Pete or maybe be the means of breaking the match altogether.

DAISY   [*severely*] Who left the gate open to entice the simple Hanrahan's through it if it wasn't yourself did it?

ROCHE   [*gaily*] 'Twas my little son did it, upon my word and honour it was and he going for a load of hay we had bought from the

Munnixes. What would a little kid of thirteen know about match-making devices? All lies and stories about our having done it deliberate.

DAISY Pish! wasn't the taycher with you behind the hedge giving you his mobile approval and the both of yeez giggling at the dodge that was played on the simple Hanrahans, the poor ignorant angashores only too delighted to give ould Munnix the thousand pounds he asked as fortune for Lena marrying his son Pete and his farm.

GUNN [*superiorily but jocosely*] I would give no man either mobile or moral approval in such a despicable transaction. I was merely seeing Mr. Roche about a terrier and he kindly invited me in to have a cup of tea—or tay to make myself clearer; and the face of our being visual observers of Mr. Hanrahan's debouche from Minnux's into Mr. Roche's five acre emerald green pasture did not make us accessories either before or after the fact.

ROCHE [*brusquely*] How could we help seeing him! Didn't he look as big as a house with his ould times of a Caroline hat on him and his beard, white and three feet long.

GUNN The scene was both pictorial and poetic. Didn't some bard or other write about a green thought in a green shade and Hanrahan must have got it standing under the tree in Munnix's field consider-ing the celerity and instinctive determination with which he made for the lovely demesne of our friend here, Mr. William Roche.

DAISY Wid Munnix pounding after him of course?

GUNN You are right, Daisy. He certainly was followed by Mr. Munnix but at a reasonable distance. Mr. Munnix didn't go the whole way, however, but paused at the gate one leg in Roche's field and one leg in his own.

DAISY [*indignantly*] A point of law! Oh, the variegated vagabone!

GUNN My dear Daisy I must really demur at your attributing the trait of vagabondage to a proud and prosperous farmer even though he may have an eye for legal niceties and has the habit of taking matters into court under the slightest provocation.

ROCHE [*hilariously*] He'd summon a woodcock for trespassing on his land if he could catch hoult of him.

DAISY [*decidedly*] There is no shame on either one or t'other of yeez not alone backing that rogue of a Munnix up but having a crow over it. [*sternly*] But, of course, you weren't so dislocated as all that.

GUNN [*puzzled*] Dislocated, eh? Oh, I twig. My charmer, do you really mean to insinuate that we were not disinterested.

DAISY [*promptly*] That's exactly what I do mean. For what did I hear [*to* ROCHE] that you got two loads of turf and a load of bog-deal as your parquisite, and the taycher's wife got six pounds of butter and a goose the next day from Mrs. Munnix. [*trenchantly*] What harm but the simple Hanrahan's being almost furriners as I might say—why it's only three years since they bought the farm they have settled on here, after coming from the County Cork.

GUNN [*jauntily*] I never yet heard of a simple person to come from Cork. Why, here in this scarcely super-ethical County of Kerry we are not supposed to possess a tithe of their congenital chicanery.

ROCHE [*gleefully*] You have knocked her out, taycher, she's beginning to flop, she's flummoxed.

DAISY No wonder I would if I was a chrishtun. Again I'm saying it—there's no shame on the both of yeez at all, at all.

ROCHE She'd make us out to be miscreeds.

GUNN Miscreants and worse, two respectable responsible men, attacking us as if we were utter debauchees. She's an iconoclast. She has no regard for reputations made.

ROCHE Are we downhearted—no sez I. And honest to boot, if we get presents it's through admiration—a compliment to the platitude of—

GUNN The rectitude.—

ROCHE Which itchude did you say there, Taycher?

GUNN Rectitude.

ROCHE A compliment to the rectitude of our way of living. So being holy, innocent and free, let us sing a song on the head of it.

DAISY Don't attempt it. Is it the guards you want to be bringing in on me.

GUNN Really Daisy, you are to maticulously pernicky in small matters.

ROCHE [*slyly*] Surprising she hasn't a notice up about it.

GUNN Like the French have in war time—*il est defendu de chanter*—no singing allowed. The guards! Why so fearful of the guards?

ROCHE [*promptly*] She's courting one of them.

GUNN Don't worry about the guards, Daisy, they like singing. They are regulars, I hear, in certain pubs along the Quays in Dublin called the great singing houses. If they don't sing in pubs in England it's because of the over-consumption of cheese which puts the damper on vocal aspirations. But their newspapers are always exhorting them to do otherwise and it's quite common to see such headlines as 'So let the people sing'.

ROCHE   I seen it myself taycher in the Sunday Despatch, so—

GUNN   [*suddenly*] So give us a hand my trusty friend—

GUNNE *and* ROCHE   [*singing*] And here's a hand o' mine. We'll drink a cup of willy-wot for the sake of auld lang syne.

For old lang syne me dee-ee-eer, for old lang syne, my dear—

DAISY   Will yeez stop! It's themselves are coming in on us whatever is bringing them—the simple Hanrahans themselves!

GUNNE *and* ROCHE   [*ignoring her. Enter* MICHAEL, MAURICE *and* MRS. HANRAHAN, *all smoking pipes*] We'll drink a cup of willy-wot for the sake of old lang syne.

GUNN   [*to the* HANRAHANS] We apologise, indeed we do.

ROCHE   [*facetiously*] Indeed and indeed we do—we apologise.

MICHAEL   [*blandly*] For why, gentlemen, should you be apologising then? Don't the birdies in the bushes be singing away for themselves and indeed it isn't apologising to no man they do be or thinking of it.

MAURICE   [*sonorously*] True for you, Michael Hanrahan, singing away for themselves they do be and no apologies.

MRS. HANRAHAN   [*searching pockets*] I am looking for that half-crown I had, for I am going to stand. The Missie is surprised I spot at seeing us—no wonder for it's thin and seldom we go into a public house, once in a way only to Miss Quinn's near the post office, where we get our rations. But it's the day of the marrying and passing here we said we'd come in and have a refresh. Where in the world is that divil of a half-crown? [*laughing*] Glory, I have it in my left hand all the time my fist closed on it. [*to* MICHAEL *and* MAURICE] Well, the both of yeez, what will ye have then.

MICHAEL   [*loudly and nonchalantly*] Bygannies, I'll have an' oul' pint of porter.

MAURICE   Me too.

MRS. HANRAHAN   [*passing piece to* DAISY] Me too.

DAISY   [*crooking her head forward, smilingly*] Are you sure it's a pint you are having also, Mrs. Hanrahan?

MRS. HANRAHAN   [*jerking up chin, vigorously and determinedly*] As sure as a gun, I am Missie, a creamy pint. [DAISY *goes to barrel at right end of shop inside counter, fills glasses and serves same, which they dispose of rapidly*]

MAURICE   Well, I am standing this time, I suppose it will be—

MICHAEL   The same again.

MRS. HANRAHAN   Ditto here.

[DAISY *serves drinks, smiling broadly*]

MICHAEL   [*as they finish drinks, with patriarchal aplomb*] Well, I am standing this time, anyway. Three more pints of porter.

MRS. HANRAHAN   [*deprecatingly*] No, I'll only have a bottle this time. Porther is very bitther.

[DAISY *goes for drinks*]

MICHAEL   [*laughing loudly*] That's always the capers with women, saying porther is bitther, grinning at it and they all the time having as big a tang for it as the next.

MAURICE   [*trenchantly*] 'Tis true for you Michael Hanrahan, they do be grinning at it and letting on they don't like it.

[DAISY *serves drinks*]

MRS. HANRAHAN   [*making a grimace, drinking in sups, decidedly*] Porther is very bitther.

MICHAEL   All the same you're as refreshed from it as we are, and now we're all in great bloom for the wedding. The hill is clear so the day will be fine though [*amusedly to teacher*] they say sir, with your larnin' you don't go by that hill at all.

GUNN   Not me, that hill is a snare, a delusion and a fraud. [*goes to door, looks up at sky, comes back*] And I can tell you, Mr. Hanrahan, that the appearance of the atmosphere denotes rain.

MICHAEL   [*gurgling with laughter*] Thank you, sir. [*trying to control laughter as all three move towards door,* MRS. HANRAHAN *and* MAURICE, *chortling*] My lovely daughter, Lena, that's getting married today don't go by it, neither. She has a round affair that she calls a barrowmayther that she goes by.

MAURICE   True for you, Michael Hanrahan, it's the barrowmayther she looks at.

MICHAEL   She could talk to you sir, for faith, she has the larnin' too. Doesn't she know Irish and French and 'tis the French she speaks to her pet dog. After coming out of hospital where I was for three months with a bloo whinsy, and seeing the little dog near the gate, 'I see, I see', sez I to the dog thinking I was saying what Lena said to him. He only gave an eye at me, cocked his tail and skedoodled.

MAURICE True for you Michael Hanrahan, the pet dog skedoodled.

MICHAEL And 'tis time we skedoodled, too, to the wedding. So, the blessing of God on you Missie and on all here.

DAISY *as the* HANRAHANS, *looking back at* GUNN *and heaving with laughter are going out*] The same to you, sir, the same to you sirs and ma'am. [*exit the* HANRAHANS. *With elbow on counter, reflectively*] With their beards and pipes and all aren't they like old children, glory be to God. When in the world did a daughter of theirs get the French, though.

GUNN I have a hunch she hasn't got a terrible lot of it. Probably about as much as Bill Quirke has of the German he learnt from the Oxford man who stayed at his fishing cottage. *Der hund ist unter dem tische*—the dog is under the table—that's all Bill knows of it now. Ah well, I suppose she can say Boulong, toulong on the Contingong and a few things like that.

ROCHE [*shrewdly*] She might know enough to civilize Pete who is all right at ploughing and digging, but in other ways is nearly as big a gom as any simple Hanrahan burring all them auld songs and tunes and side-cracks—

GUNN Wise cracks.

ROCHE And wise-cracks that he has picked up from the radio.

DAISY [*looking out window*] There he is outside getting off the car. He is letting his da and ma go and he is coming in. Faith, he's got up in style for the marrying. Anybody to look at him now without knowing would take him for a half-gent [*enter* PETE] Good morning to you, Pete Munnix.

PETE [*grandly*] Good morning to you, Daisy. Good day to all of yeez. I see the Hanrahans going up the town after coming out of here. Did they stand?

ROCHE They stood to themselves. That's all the standing we see them do.

PETE The poor things are too ignorant to know the attyteeket of a day of a wedding. I'll have a glass of 5 star Sandeman, Daisy, as I feel shilly and [*nodding to* ROCHE *and* GUNN] they'll have what they will have.

ROCHE *and* GUNN Two Redbreasts.

PETE 'Tisn't making little of them ould people the Hanrahans, I'd be [*to* GUNN] Master, you know that, but the world knows they haven't got the—the—

III

9

GUNN *Savoir faire—*savvy for short.

PETE [*cutely*] I know that word you said first, taycher, savoury. I heard it on the wireless a week ago. [DAISY *serves drinks*] Well, here's luck to ye, and to the nate girl I'm getting married to to-day.

GUNN She is indeed a nate girl as you put it, Pete.

PETE [*enthusiastically*] She's nate out abye us. It's only three months since I seen her first, I passing by in the horse-and-car on the road and she in her garden waggin' herself to and fro in her hammock. Well, master, I got a dart from the eye of cupidity and ever after the thought of her eyes and her face and her hair wouldn't leave me, I her pure slave, glory be to God!

GUNN [*slyly*] And when those few words are said to-day by the priest over the pair of you, you'll be her slave for the rest of your life.

PETE [*promptly*] And her willing slave I'd be for forty lives if I had them. Upon my seconds Daisy, she has the whitest teeth I ever seen in a girl—her ivories she calls 'em.

DAISY [*drily*] I suppose she takes care to give a little laugh now and then to show them off.

PETE [*joyously*] She does! In my happiness I tried to make a little pome about her. I'll recite it:

Praised be the day I first did spy my beauteous Lena Hanrahan
Lovely as Vaynus, chaste as Diana she certainly was then;
Her ears were small, her eyes were blue, her
Face was pink and white and [*with far-away look*]
Mary, Mary, quite contrary, how does your garden grow, with silver bells and—
there is that ould rhyme always coming into my head, and if you paid me I couldn't now think of the finish of the verse about Lena. I pulled myself up though, taycher.

GUNN You did, definitely, though it was a near thing.

PETE 'Twas different when I was a youngster. I'd do th'ould rhyme without thinking. Maybe, Master, you know that pome about 'On Linden when the sun was low'?

GUNN [*drily*] Time I did know it.

PETER My aunt Liz who learnt a share—she was in the fifth book at school—got me to recite it wanst for two praishts back from Austrailway (*jauntily, pulling out comb from pocket and combing back front locks from forehead*], brothers of Liz, uncles of mine. I knew

the pome by heart and was getting on finely till I came to the last
spasm, and I not thinking a whack, what came out but—

Mary, Mary, quite contrary
How does your garden grow.
With silver bells and cockle shells
And fair maids all in a row.

My Aunt Liz in a fright clapped her hands and let a little scrame
that went up the chimley. But [*shrewdly*] it was all right, Master.
The two praishts they gave me a half-crown each, and I could
swear it to you, they laughed for nearly half-an-hour.

GUNN   No need to swear it, or even to emphasise it, not even if you
told me they laughed or chuckled for another half-hour to boot.

DAISY   [*who has been looking out window at extreme left over 'snug'*]
There's your beauty Lena, Pete, in the motor with her sister from
Dublin and a man with her.

PETE   [*astounded*] A man with her! [*runs to door, turns back laughs*]
That's not a man; that's the other sister from Dublin. Didn't I
think she was a man, too, the first time I seen her and she riding a
horse around the farm. They made a holy show of me at my mistake
when I called her 'Sir' and the dame herself nearly died wid the
dint of laughing. 'Tisn't a trouser she calls what she has on at all,
Daisy, but smacks.

GUNN   [*slyly*] Sure it wasn't slacks?

PETE   God knows Taycher, you might be right. It could be slacks.

GUNN   [*gaily*] Smacks, stacks, slacks—well, what about it? Why
should we worry even if she called them early in the morning.

PETE   [*reflectively and decidedly*] It was slacks taycher, it was. I
recollect it now—slacks, but faith 'tis a rale trouser she wears when
she goes galloping around the Phaynix Park. Well, so long to yeez.
[*turns around and makes his exit rapidly but awkwardly*]

DAISY   [*putting elbows on counter, severely*] Slacks! A quare get-up
entirely for a girl coming to this part of the country.

GUNN   [*suavely*] I agree with you its rather *outre*. Not that I shouldn't
find a sort of malicious pleasure in her shocking the aborigines men,
those whom I shall term—ungrammatically—the *reductio ad
absurdum* of bucolic intransigeance—those babes and sucklings her
people the ineffable Hanrahans who seemed to consider themselves
quite entitled to indulge in gurgles of risibility over my quite
ordinary remark or a current meteorological phenomenon—

ROCHE [*gaily*] That stung you, taycher.

GUNN Thereby and *ipso facto* obviously imagined they were raising themselves to the mental level of, and possessing an equal modicum of the tantalising conceit of their smug, circum-ambient complers who, whenever they hear anything from me outside the purview of their diurnal concepts, immediately adopt an attitude of condescending pity and look at me like early Christians.

DAISY [*blithely*] The people don't appreciate you taycher the way they should.

GUNN [*frivolously*] Thou hast spoken, Aunt Sophia.

DAISY But isn't it said that a project has no honour in its own country [*short pause*], or is it a prodigy I mean?

GUNN Don't worry about trifles, Daisy. In any event I don't consider myself a prophet, so carry on, Daisy, I think you were going to say something else?

DAISY [*cutely*] I was. I wisht to say I heard there was a big thought of you in other places and that they call you Ireland's own National Taycher.

GUNN I blush. Though I doubt if it is with pride or even with pleasure I regret to say. But time is slipping and there's a malicious gleam in Daisy's eye [*going towards door followed by* ROCHE] she'd like to have us be late; she begrudges us the fun she knows we'll have at the wedding of the refined Lena with her French and all, and the one and only Pete Munnix.

ROCHE I'm thinking, Taycher, that gleam in Daisy's eye has more of fun than malefactionnea in it. I noticed it for a bit as if she was tempted to tell me something maybe what happened between Lena and the sow-pig in the garden. As sure as a gun that's what's pinching you Daisy?

DAISY [*smiling, facetiously and brusquely*] It might and it mightn't.

ROCHE 'Twas from Dan Martin I had it, Taycher, a quiet little man that wouldn't tell a lie and be bothered from his wife that's the whole boss with her badgering at their two common daughters every day of the week because they aren't lady-like as Lena Hanrahan. And that was the surprise he got he told me and he passing one day by the Hanrahan's place and heard my damsel, Lena, having a tally-ho with the sow-pig that broke into her flower-garden.

GUNN [*loftily*] I shouldn't mind that. An obstreperous sow-pig would upset the equilibristic decorum in a duchess or even in a—

I don't say it disrespectfully—or even in a Reverend Mother.

ROCHE   Oh, Dan didn't mind her shouting at the sow-pig neither nor even swearing at the pig, Master, but what flummoxed him was to hear expressions come from her that females around here don't use at all, that in the usual—the regular—the common—the—the—

GUNN   Things that ordinarily speaking—

ROCHE   That's right, Taycher, that's what he said things that ordinary speaking, sez he, you'd expect would only come from the mouth of an ould soldier.

DAISY   [*laughingly*] He! He! He!

GUNN   What a shock for an old Victorian. Though apparently, incredible as it may seem, it doesn't appear to have shocked Daisy. You're right, Bill, she surely heard about Lena's ebullition in the garden.

DAISY   [*firmly*] If I heard about her ablution itself, it isn't joining in with either of yez about it I'd be, after the roguery ye did on her poor old simple beardy-puss of a da. So that's that for yeez.

ROCHE   One in the kisser for each of us. Let us scramble while we are alive. They say a keeping beauty is as dangerous as a tiger.

GUNN   It's a boa-constrictor you're thinking of not a sleeping beauty. But a wide awake beauty behind a counter suffused with virtuous indignation might—

ROCHE   Might pelt a bottle.

DAISY   And I'd like to pelt a bottle at something this minute.

GUNN   Yes, let us scramble. *Au'voir*, Daisy.

DAISY   [*coming rapidly to entrance door from behind counter through 'snug' waving hands*] Ye don't deserve it, but all the same I'll say good luck to the pair of yeez.

CURTAIN

ACT II

The scene is the interior of the Munnix's kitchen. At right, entrance door. At left of door large window beside which is a long deal table. To left of table door leading to bedroom. At extreme left fireplace, chairs, stool, etc., an armchair being placed in front of table. At extreme right a large dresser.

As curtain rises Eileen Munnix is discovered holding on to back of armchair evidently in a state of expectancy. Enter Munnix, senior, Mrs. Munnix, Pete, Gunn and Roche severally, followed by Lena, her father and mother with Maurice Hanrahan bringing up the rear. They lead her ceremoniously to armchair and place her in it. All three (Michael, Maurice and Mrs. Hanrahan) then start weeping copiously which reaches to a crescendo of howling. Mrs. Hanrahan seeming almost in a state of collapse from emotion.

MRS. MUNNIX [*painfully affected, appealingly*] Don't, don't, Mrs. Hanrahan. I beg of you. After all, you don't live but a quarter of a mile away, and 'tis of ten you'll be meeting your lovely daughter.

MICHAEL [*tragically*] Our hearts are broken to be having her leaving us. She was a saint in the house.

MRS. HANRAHAN [*still weeping*] That's what she was, indeed, Mrs. Munnix.

MAURICE [*deeply moved*] 'Tis true for you, Michael Hanrahan, it's a pure saint she was in the house itself.

EILEEN [*butting in to* MRS. HANRAHAN] And you can see, ma'am, the process-server's [*pulls herself up as her father and mother make frantic signs and look daggers at her*] You can see the high green field from your place and see Lena too when she walks in it. And, maybe, she'd take her hammock there to have a swing for herself.

MICHAEL And a beauteous vision we will see if she goes a hammocking in that lovely green field.

MAURICE [*with emotion*] That's true for you, Michael Hanrahan; it's a lovely picture she and her hammot will make in the middle of the green field.

MICHAEL But a marrying is a marrying, so we'll have to be leaving you, darling Lena.

LENA [*acidly, as they embrace her theatrically*] Good-bye Pop, good-bye, Mom, good-bye Uncle Maurice—so long—so long.

EILEEN [*to* PETE *and* LENA, *as* HANRAHANS *move towards door*]
To bed, to bed!

LENA [*amusedly, shrieking with pretended horror*] Tiens! Tiens!
howld me Michael, or something will give!

MRS. MUNNIX [*soothingly to* LENA] Don't mind Eileen, Lena, she
was her grandmother's—Bid Horan's—pet and has a whole bibful
of that ould woman's quare sayings. I bet now Lena, that you have
plenty of sense and understand that the little girl is too young to
know what she is saying.

GUNN [*facetiously to* MRS. MUNNIX] I don't know ma'am, that
Eileen's phraseological explision is really so queer as you seem to
think. Have I not read something like it in Shakespeare? Have I or
have I not? However, I can assure you that rare old Ben Jonson
wouldn't have turned a hair at hearing it. People weren't so
finicky in Ben's time—they had beer for their breakfast instead
of tea.

MRS. MUNNIX [*decidedly*] Ah, taycher, she was a very droll ould
woman was Bids Horan. Indeed, th'ould people generally were very
quare in their way of talking.

MICHAEL [*turning around, speaking from near doorway*] They were
quare and curus, th'ould people. But, faith, they did their share of
work. 'Twas them drained all the land and 'twas them died of the
rheumatiz.

MAURICE [*earnestly*] True for you, Michael Hanrahan, 'twas them
drained all the land and 'twas them died of the rehumatiz.

MICHAEL They were very quare but they had their own sense.
They were full of tricks trying to get at the blind side of landlords,
agents and sub-agents and they all rack-rented. And, by gannies,
if they were ignorant, they were witty.

GUNN [*suavely*] Veritable experts, Mr. Hanrahan, so to speak, in
the art of the intellectual double entender.

MICHAEL [*trying to control laughter*] You are talking fine, sir.

MAURICE [*ditto*] True for you, Michael Hanrahan, he's talking
fine.

MRS. HANRAHAN [*ditto*] Magnifeek sir, ah, but it's grand the larnin'
and so it is. [*exit* HANRAHANS]

ROCHE [*glibly*] Don't get stomached, Taycher, 'twas no lie for Mrs.
Hanrahan, it's grand the larnin'.

GUNN [*humorously*] It is if you haven't got it. Having it you find out that it is merely a vehicle to enable you to harmonize the ego with its surroundings, to bring so to speak, the intensive into proper forces with the extensive.

MRS. MUNNIX [*utterly puzzled, then suddenly to* GUNN *and* ROCHE] You'll be having something before you go [*to* MUNNIX *and* PETE] and you'll be having something too [*to* LENA] I didn't like to be offering your people anything, Lena, they're old and having that young horse. But maybe, you'll have a little tint yourself, Lena.

LENA [*affably*] *Volunties, maman.*

MRS. MUNNIX Eileen, get the bottle, it's above in the room. [*to* LENA] the room that's to be yours and Pete's, agragil.

LENA [*blithely*] *Compree, maman.* [EILEEN *returns with bottle of whiskey*]

MRS. MUNNIX [*to* MUNNIX *as she fills out drinks*] If it isnt' deaf, I'm getting but I can't understand a word the darling girl is saying.

ROCHE [*who has gone to door after having taken his drink*] Well, such going I never see! They came at a fair pace, but it's no fair pace with them going back but galloping like sixty!

MRS. MUNNIX [*in alarm*] Glory, it couldn't be the young horse is running away with them.

ROCHE There's no running away, don't I see ould Hanrahan belting and whipping her on.

[EILEEN *leads* LENA *quietly to room and returns*]

MRS. MUNNIX [*clasping hands*] The grief must be effecting the poor honest, decent man.

EILEEN [*interposing*] How could it be grief, mother, and they laughing their lights out. I saw through the window th'ould man with the berd especially making a holy show laughing his mouth open that wide he could nearly swallow a pig and you could see his teeth. He has high teeth like a horse.

MRS. MUNNIX [*smiling*] Just like babes they are, one minute bawling and squalling and the next scramin' with laughter.

[ROCHE *who has gone out returns looking amused*]

ROCHE A man from Abbeyfeale, one Tom Daly, wants to see you quick, Martin Munnix. It's the same man that was fined ten shillings lately because of his cow breaking into ould Hanrahan's rape.

MUNNIX [*gruffly*] What has that got to do with me? 'Twasn't I summoned him but ould Hanrahan.

ROCHE [*slyly*] Better talk to him anyway. He is looking very humorous and he wants a word with you, too, taycher, and he has something else to say to myself.

[*exit* ROCHE, GUNN *and* MUNNIX. *Meanwhile* EILEEN *has handed a lighted candle in a sconce to* PETE *as he goes into room*]

MRS. MUNNIX [*sharply*] A candle and this a fine sunny day. There is no sense in it, not to mind the expense.

EILEEN [*sweetly*] Sure, mother, it only cost a pinny and it wouldn't be respectable the day of a marrying to go into a room without a candle and only a small little windy in it.

MRS. MUNNIX [*going to room door which has been closed by* PETE] Put it out, Pete, before you go to bed, agragil; you might forget it and burn the house. You'll put it out.

PETE [*in room, in voice which sounds far away*] All right, mum!

[MRS. MUNNIX *goes to dresser and starts re-arranging the crockery.* EILEEN *seats herself on sugaun chair and makes some show at knitting. Suddenly room door opens, and* PETE, *coatless, bursts down as if panic-stricken*]

PETE [*in loud, frightened voice*] Ma! Ma!

MRS. MUNNIX [*turning around*] In the name of all that's good Pete, what is it?

PETE [*darkly*] She has a wooden leg.

MRS. MUNNIX [*with gurgle of horror*] Oh, glory!

PETE [*rapidly*] 'Tisn't her own teeth she has got at all. Without saying yes, I, or no, didn't she put her hand in her mouth opposite me, pulled them out and placed them on the shelf.

MRS. MUNNIX Oh, hierna!

PETE [*drearily*] She has no hair.

MRS. MUNNIX In the name of goodness what has she then?

PETE [*in hollow tones*] A wig!

MRS. MUNNIX [*throwing her arms around* PETE'S *neck*] Me poor child, me poor darlint child.

[*re-enter noisily* MUNNIX, GUNN *and* ROCHE]

MUNNIX Stop your hillabilloo, Eleanor. The man from Abbeyfeale has told us all and we are going in a deputation to the rogues to force the old villain Hanrahan, to give us at least another thousand pounds as a solarium—as a soladium—

GUNN As a solatium—

MUNNIX As a solatium for the infernal wrong he has done on us.

[*harshly*] The fine lady will have to come to. [*to* PETE] You can bring her.

MRS. MUNNIX [*drearily*] What can the poor boy do with her and she in bits by him above in the bed.

MUNNIX [*fiercely*] Let him put her together again. [*to* PETE] Up in the room at wanst with you, I'm telling you, and put her together again. And you'll have to hyse her on your back as we are going by the short cut and your duchess with her game leg can't climb ditches. [PETE *obediently goes into room*]

MRS. MUNNIX [*looking after* PETE, *wringing hands*] The poor boy, the poor crathur.

MUNNIX [*to* EILEEN] You run off and tell the skaymers there's a deputation coming to them. I hear the characters go to bed at seven and get up at five so tell them to remain up till the deputation comes or we'll break in the door.

[*exit* EILEEN *rapidly*]

MRS. MUNNIX [*woefully*] Who'd ever believe they'd be like that!

MUNNIX The man from Abbeyfeale wouldn't be surprised and he had no doubt it was delibert—dd—

GUNN Deliberate.

MUNNIX Deliberate and that 'twas delibertal also what they thought was done in innocence, the Hanrahans selling the kicking horse to the taycher and the cow wid the blind eye to the process-server.

GUNN [*lightly*] Beg pardon, the civil bill officer.

MUNNIX [*drily to* ROCHE] I beg pardon, civil bill officer, but the man from Abbeyfeale would swear 'twas done deliberate—I mean delibert.

GUNN [*facetiously*] So he would, and, if true, represents a revelation of really shocking chicanery.

ROCHE [*ditto*] Shocking chicanery and we keeping silent all the time, the taycher about the kicking horse and myself about the cow with the blind eye we ashamed to let the people know we bought the like, never suspecting we had been diddled by Simple Hanrahans either deliberate or delibert.

MUNNIX Yours are small things compared with my tragedy, but it will furcify—forgify—

GUNN Fortify—

MUNNIX Fortify the deputation we being all in the same hoax.

GUNN All in the same boat.

MUNNIX [*testily*] All in the same hoax. That's how I heard it H.O.X.E. hoax, what's wrong with it?

GUNN Nothing so far as I can see. Indeed, in the circumstance, it could well be that yours is the more correct expression.

MUNNIX [*grudgingly, after some reflection*] No taycher, I'll leave it to you—the tongue must be getting a bit skiddey by me on account of the trouble that's on me. Moreover, I never do be quite sure of myself about one of them things my brother in Californy used to call a metaphosphorous.

GUNN [*musingly*] A metamorphosis? Quite sure he didn't say aphorism?

MUNNIX Absolutely sure. And he is a smart man [*meaningly*] has plenty of his share of learning, but better than that spent thirteen years in Californy. Metaphosphorous is what he said and metaphosphorous is the word.

GUNN [*gaily*] Hear, hear, loud cheers and laughter.

MUNNIX That will do now, Mr. Jaymary Gunn (*to* MRS. MUNNIX] But, it's all right, the taycher is to be the spokeshafe of the party—

GUNN The spokesman of the deputation—

MUNNIX The spokesman of the deputation. He has everything off tip-tap.

GUNN Pit-pat.

MUNNIX I thought it was tip-tap.

GUNN Oh, tip-tap will do well enough.

MUNNIX Everything off pit-pat, tip tap. [*as* LENA *and* PETE *come down from room, caustically*] Ah, here comes the bride!

LENA [*seating herself in arm-chair, pertly*] Kayss, Keely-a dona?

MUNNIX [*savagely*] What nonsense are going on with about killing a donkey? Acting the ape, eh? Though, indeed, it must have been well tutored you were by your ould vagabone of a father. [*trenchantly*] And having mentioned him isn't it the bitter thought now comes of me of having—of having devoured—of having digoured—

GUNN Of having ignored—

MUNNIX Of having ignored me own poor ould father's advice never to trust anyone with an out-of-character big berd it's for to consale something forbolical—something dis—

GUNN Something diabolical.

MUNNIX Something diabolical—them were the words he said.

LENA [*sweetly*] Just fancy, and mother and Uncle Maurice so proud of father's big beard.

GUNN [*smilingly*] Lena, you should have given it a better term. Being your father's, you should have referred to it as his extensive and snowy hirsute patriarchal appendage.

LENA [*laughing*] Of course, I should, Mr. Gunn.

MUNNIX [*roughly*] Oh, they're proud of it are they? and the uncle I spine—I pine—

GUNN I opine—

MUNNIX I opine as big a rogue as your father with whiskers as long as the other's berd and an ould moustache three times the size of Sir Sidney's.

GUNN Do you really mean the old aristocrat in 'Mutt and Jeff'?

MUNNIX The very man.

LENA [*suddenly to* MUNNIX] Voo zayte commeek.

MUNNIX [*puzzled to* MRS. MUNNIX] What is she saying, at all, at all?

MRS. MUNNIX [*sourly*] I don't know what she's saying if it isn't something about you're having at pig's cheek.

GUNN [*interposing*] Sorry Mrs. Munnix, but I am afraid I cannot agree with you. My acquaintance with the Gallic vernacular is not very extensive, but I think the young lady means to convey that your beloved husband is slightly weak in the head.

MUNNIX Is that all she said! If she said I was a complete fool, she'd be nearer the mark and the way I let myself be had by her dersert sursite—high-suit—

GUNN Hirsute—

MUNNIX By her hirsute father.

MRS. MUNNIX [*sharply to* LENA] You with your glib back-chat.

LENA [*pointing finger at* MRS. MUNNIX, *gesticulating with assumed fierceness*] Cochonne de vieux fam, debarrassez par lah, debarassez par lah!

MRS. MUNNIX What bad thing is she saying to me now, taycher?

GUNN Merely requesting you to have the things cleared off that little table at your back.

MRS. MUNNIX What sneering has she! Doesn't she know we hadn't time to be doing everything, put about and it a day of a wedding. But [*to* LENA] to continoo, you and your glib back-chat instead of showing some remorse for being the ruination and corruption of

my poor saintly son [*weeping*] the most innocent boy in the parish;
just thirty years of age that innocent indeed that he didn't know a
man from a woman till he led you to the altar this very day.

LENA [*acidly*] Well, my good lady so far as I am aware, he is still
in his state of pristine innocence.

MRS. MUNNIX [*suspiciously*] I don't know but its immoral you're
talking.

LENA I don't know, either, so we're quits mother-in-law.

MRS. MUNNIX No shame on you or signs of shame, and now it's
plain to me the trops and wiles you laid to entice my darling son.

LENA [*with pretended anger*] Pardon me, Mrs. Munnix, but I really
must resent this soft or hard impeachment. Pete, himself will, I
think, admit that for weeks he was moving in my vicinity without
my being aware of his presence, peeping at me through the bushes.

PETE Oh, that's God's truth, mother. For weeks she didn't know I
was there at all, at all.

MRS. MUNNIX [*pityingly*] Go on wid yeez, yar poor silly child!
It would take a lot to persuade me she hadn't spotted you out of the
corner of her eye and was seducing you unbeknownst.

GUNN That's very shrewd of you Mrs. Munnix. That's like something King Solomon would say and really did say thousands of
years ago. Which shows, as the French say, *plus ca change*—

LENA [*interposing laughingly and rapidly*] Plus c'est la meme chose.

MUNNIX [*interrupting, gruffly*] Here, there's enough of this cooter-
foodling. [*to* PETE] You start first. What waiting have you man, and
what looking have you at me, but hyse her on your back and march
off with her like a bowld soper boy.

LENA [*to* MUNNIX, *half coquettishly, half tearfully*] Oh you horrid,
bold, cruel, grizzly, shameless old man.

MRS. MUNNIX [*fiercely*] What crime is it, you hussey, to be on
Pete's back and he your lawful married husband.

LENA [*caustically*] Married and even churched.

MUNNIX [*losing patience, to* PETE *who has not yet made a move*] What
gaping have you at me but ketch her. [*to* MRS. MUNNIX] If it's a
help he wants we'll give him a help. [PETE *takes hold of* LENA'S
hands. MUNNIX *and wife help hoist her on his back*] On with you now
in front.

LENA [*as* PETE *hauls her towards exit, half looking over shoulder with
a bleary little smile*] Oh, crickey! Oh, shocking, shocking, as Made-

123

moisells from Armentieres said when she sat on a pin. Oh, shocking, shocking!

[*exit* PETE *with* LENA]

ROCHE [*aside to* GUNN *whilst* MRS. MUNNIX *has gone to corner fixing herself up for departure,* MUNNIX *observing her*] I think more of that dame than what I did. She didn't take it half as tragic as another might have done in the circumstances.

GUNN [*superiorily*] Even if she bawled and screamed however pathetic it wouldn't be tragic, tragedy as the Greeks well know, having really a conventional mode of representation alien to our stratum in Society being properly applicable only to elevated characters such as kings and queens, etc., it being denied to them the consolation of Bunyan's under dog, saint or humbug or whatever he was who perpetrated the bland generalisation that he that was low need fear no fall.

MUNNIX [*losing patience with* GUNN *but speaking crossly to* MRS. MUNNIX] Are you ready yet?

GUNN [*continuing, loftily*] I was speaking, of course, and the obverse of the medal for, paradoxical as it may seem the acid test of a genuine tragedy is that it lends itself particularly to ribaldry as by God! good old Harry Fielding well illustrated by his skit on the *Oedipus Rex* in *Tom Jones*. Lena's case is therefore merely pathetic, for the fact of her being elevated on Pete's back by no means raises her to the sphere of tragedy.

MUNNIX [*suddenly and roughly*] Are we all ready at last?

GUNN We're perfectly ready, Mr. Munnix. But your wife doesn't seem anxious to move. She seems upset. There is an anxious look in her eye.

ROCHE She's struck still-stock.

GUNN Yes, she's standing stock-still. My dear Mrs. Munnix have you made or are you about to make a *volto face*? Have the cords of your dear old maternal heart been struck by the tragedy—by the er —pathos of the scene?

MRS. MUNNIX [*rapidly*] No sich a thing. As if I'd give wan tuppenny ticket about that dame and her tragic or whatever the gap is about. What's worrying me is leaving the house empty before the little girl comes back.

ROCHE Don't be troubled woman of the house. Myself and the taycher are champion walkers. We'll wait for the little girl and over-take yourself and your hubby before you reach the Hanrahans.

MUNNIX   A very good objection—a very good selection—I mean a very good subjection, Mr. Roche.

GUNN   A very good suggestion, indeed.

MUNNIX   [*testily*] Subjection I said.

MRS. MUNNIX   [*to* MUNNIX] It's you that's no delaying, arguifying with the taycher over conundrums. [*goes to door*] It's very much obliged we are to you, Civil Bill Officer.

MUNNIX   [*following her, sententiously*] It's very much obliged we are to you entiredly, Civil Bill Officer.

[*exit* MUNNIXES]

ROCHE   [*going to dresser*] They wouldn't be so obliged if they knew what I was after. That oul' wizert or a woman didn't pour a quarter out of the bottle, but it's so much the better for us. I don't know where she put the glasses but the cups will do. Whiskey is as good out of a cup as out of a glass. [*takes both of bottles and pours contents into two cups*] Now, taycher you know the reason for my bilacrity.

GUNN   I know the reason for your alacrity all right, but I refuse to understand or even appreciate your gesture in stealing the people's whiskey.

ROCHE   Stealing be damned. It's only purblind.

GUNN   Purloined! that's just as bad.

ROCHE   Pinched then, let it be. [*drinks and hands second cup to* GUNN]

GUNN   [*decidedly, shaking head but taking hold of cup*] Nothing doing.

ROCHE   Now, taycher, that woman should have offered us another drink it being a wedding day and we going in a deputation. But she forgot it with the fuss that was on her. Let us be pretending to ourselves that she did anyway.

GUNN   Let us be pretending to ourselves! You want to entice me with the insinuation that nothing is good or bad but thinking makes it so. Avaunt thee, Satan! Am I not a teacher and an instructor of youth, a moral expositor? You scarify me at my most sensitive. You insult my highest principles, especially when, in placing this temptation in my way, you know very well that if I don't succumb to it I shall be regretting I have not done so before we are half way to the Hanrahans.

ROCHE   Drink it up before the little girl comes and catches us which would be a bigger disgrace for you in your toploftiness than for me a mere process-civil bill officer.

GUNN [*holding cup at arm's length*] Take it away, take it away. [*as* ROCHE *makes gesture to take cup. draws back arm*] Well, wait a bit. Fight temptation, yes, but there is no good in half fighting it, so here goes and by Jingo! I'll banish it. [*gulps down drink*]

ROCHE [*taking back cups to dresser*] I'll put the cups on the saucers in the dresser. Cups on dressers are supposed to be washed so the little girl will leave them alone—I'll turn them upside down in the saucer to make a surety a certainty.

GUNN But they weren't turned upside down before so the change might make her suspicious. Why not give them a rinse?

ROCHE I see no water to give them a rinse. She'll never spot the change. And I'll put the empty bottle under the little bucket on the lower shelf of the dresser so that with her oothamawlin' about the house the little girl is certain to pull the bucket and break the bottle on the flags. She'll never be suspecting us but in her panic will be thinking of nothing but how to conceal the damage from her parents. What I don't know about the capers of little girls isn't worth knowing—no wonder, with my six of them. But, isn't it cute?

GUNN It's more than cute—it's diabolically subtle.

ROCHE [*as they move towards exit*] I'd be more subtle if I had the larnin'. Larnin' comes in very handy, even in swallowing one's principles, I mean one's whiskey, taycher.

GUNN [*grimly*] Oh, thou elephantine cynic.

[*enter* EILEEN *suddenly.* GUNN *and* ROCHE *are taken aback*]

ROCHE [*recovering himself*] Bolt the door when we leave, little girl, to keep out the boogie man.

GUNN And be looking out the window at the fowl and the pig. Be looking at the big cock strutting so proudly on the ash-heap. And when you are tired of looking out the window, read that nice little story in your story book. Will you?

EILEEN [*obediently*] I will, sir. [*they go out.* EILEEN *bolts door*] I will, sir, sez I, but what else could I say and the man talking apish. [*she gets busy at re-settling chairs, etc. Finally, comes to fireplace and stands with hands behind back. She looks towards dresser, her gaze becoming gradually more intent at the place where the bottle had been. After a pause, putting finger on lower lip*] Paddy in the railway was shtanding on a shto-an; up comes an injun and br-r-r-eaks all his bo-ans. [*goes to dresser, takes cup off saucer and smells it gleefully*] Fee, faw, fum, I smell the blood of an Irishman. [*smells the second cup*] Fee, faw fum [*looks at bucket suspiciously*] ha! [*replaces cup, goes and carefully inspects bucket, after short pause cautiously lifts bucket, places it on floor and takes hold of bottle. Holds it up to light and sees that it is empty. Comes to front of stage holding bottle in hands. Triumphantly*] Ha-hah, Sherlock Holmes, Sherlock Holmes!

CURTAIN

ACT III

The scene is the Hanrahan's kitchen. At back fireplace. To left near fireplace a huge, full-length mirror. Opposite mirror at right also near fireplace a large arm-chair in which Michael Hanrahan is seated when curtain rises. To right of arm-chair a stool. Mrs. Hanrahan being seated on end near Michael, and Maurice on other end. To left of mirror a table and window. Further to left, entrance door. Behind Mrs. Hanrahan and Maurice is a clevy affixed to the wall, on which are cups and bric-a-brac. Further to right is a barometer.

MICHAEL [*taking pipe from mouth, dully*] There's some noise going on outside. It could be that deputation.

[MAURICE *rises from stool suddenly, upsetting* MRS. HANRAHAN— *who, however, re-settles herself rapidly without demur—and goes to door. Turns around*]

MAURICE [*taking pipe from mouth, gravely*] 'Tis true for you, Michael Hanrahan, it is the deputation. They be coming in. [*re-seats himself on stool. All three puff tobacco vigorously. After a short pause* MICHAEL *again takes pipe from mouth and spits at mirror with a loud tit.* MRS. HANRAHAN *and* MAURICE *follow suit,* MICHAEL'S *spit being the highest and* MRS. HANRAHAN'S *the lowest. Enter* PETE *with* LENA *on his back, whom he deposits on floor, followed severally by* MUNNIX, MRS. MUNNIX, GUNN *and* ROCHE]

MUNNIX [*rapidly*] And now, let us make short work of the job. As we arranged the bell—

GUNN —the ball—

MUNNIX —the ball or the bell, it doesn't matter which—the ball or the bell is to you taycher and you having everything off tip-tap, tap-tip, pit-pat.

GUNN I have, or rather I should say, I had, for I believe its coming on that old complaint of mine an access of vocal frigidity.

ROCHE [*laughing loudly*] Ha! ha! ha!

MUNNIX [*grumpily*] 'Tisn't thinking of renagging me you are with your nonsense about an abscess of stupidity. Wasn't the whole thing to begin on the legacy—on the illegacy—on the ill—

GUNN —on the inadequacy.

MUNNIX —on the inadekasy of the cod pro kid. I mean the kid pro cod.

GUNN [*with dignity*] Of the quid pro quo. What Mr. Munnix means, Mr. Hanrahan, is that, while denying that he was in any way instrumental in putting across you a wrong idea as to the ownership of a certain parcel of land, the said wrong idea, however suspicious you may or may not be as to how you became possessed of it, would, on nowise, represent a *quid pro quo* in juxtaposition with what Mr. Munnix considers the monstrous injury you have done to him.

MUNNIX [*vigorously*] To fit—to bit—to kit—[*waving index finger wildly at* GUNN *who has turned about talking in dumb show to* ROCHE] Taycher, taycher!

GUNN [*turning around*] Sorry Mr. Munnix—to wit.

MUNNIX To wit: damages diablorous—

GUNN —Damages dolorous.

MUNNIX —Damages dolorous, which will be hereinbefore and hereinbewhich speculated on if ness.

GUNN [*blandly*] Quite so; which will be specified hereinafter if necessary. In other words, Mr. Hanrahan, Mr. Munnix will accept the sum of one thousand pounds from you as the minimum in settlement of his claim. His original claim was for fifteen hundred pounds, but he has chivalrously deducted a whole five hundred pounds from it, not because you could legally advance anything in the nature of a *quid pro quo*, but as a *solatium* to your wounded feelings, if any, Mr. Munnix for the very good reasons advanced by the man from Abbeyfeale believing that you were under no illusion whatever with respect to the ownership of a certain green field.

MICHAEL [*looking about him, stupidly*] What green field sir, is it, the triangle?

MRS. HANRAHAN [*smiling*] I'd say it was the big green field you walked the day of the matchmaking, Michael, the greenest field I ever see, except our own—inch near the thundering big river we lived by in the County Cork.

GUNN [*smilingly*] A thundering big river—the Lee or the Blackwater?

MRS. HANRAHAN [*definitely*] Well then, neither of them was the name of it. I had it on the tip of my tongue, but it's gone again. What in the name of all that's good was the name of it, at all, at all.

MICHAEL I can't think from Adam what was the name of it. It's gone out of my head complate.

MAURICE   True for you, Michael Hanrahan, it's gone out our heads, complate.

MUNNIX   [*suddenly and savagely*] Dub—dub—

MRS. MUNNIX   [*catching him*] Didn't the doctor tell you not to get excited and you having the high blood pressure. Will you be quiet?

GUNN   It is quite understandable, Mr. Munnix, your impatience at this divagation. But, being a schoolmaster, you'll comprehend my being intrigued at the idea of their being a thundering big river in County Cork the existence of which I have been hitherto unaware. Mrs. Henrahan, do please try again to recall the *cognomen* of this fluid thunderer much bigger of course than our own river here— no mean salmon river by the way—except the Feale.

MRS. HANRAHAN   [*scornfully*] Ten times bigger—twenty times bigger—thirty times bigger than the Feale.

GUNN   [*jocosely*] Good gracious, Mrs. Hanrahan, how have you forgotten the name of this stupendous stream?

MRS. HANRAHAN   [*suddenly and triumphantly*] I have it—the river Shannon, sir.

GUNN   [*suavely*] I am sorry, my dear lady, but I have to charge you with a slight error in nomenclature and for the excellent reason that the river Shannon does not run through the County Cork.

MRS. HANRAHAN   Indeed, sir that's what everybody called it.

MICHAEL   The woman is right, sir. Didn't we see it with our own two eyes running through it, and it wasn't running away from it it was at all, sir, but running fair and square a big bowld river right through the middle of it.

MAURICE   True for you, Michael Hanrahan, a big bowld river running right through the middle of it.

MICHAEL   [*slyly*] At the same time, Morisheen, even if we did see it running through the County Cork, with our own two eyes, 'tisn't contradicting larnin' we'd be.

MRS. HANRAHAN   [*humorously*] Indeed, what a nice thing we'd do.

MAURICE   [*ditto*] True for you Michael Hanrahan, 'tisn't contradicting larnin' we'd be.

GUNN   Once more I blush and again neither with pleasure nor with pride. But, *retournous a nos moutons*—

MUNNIX   [*losing all patience, gruffly*] What has this got to do with bringing things down to sticklebacks, taycher.

GUNN   [*evenly*] I am getting down to tin-tacks, Mr. Munnix, but the circumlocution was unavoidable. And, Mr. Munnix, when we are up against a psychological problem such as our good friends, the Hanrahans, undoubtedly present, the longest way round is often the shortest way home. In any event, one of your propositions, namely, that they are filled with the intrinsic double-dealing attribute, probably wrongly, to the natives of County Cork, is completely thrown overboard, for, notwithstanding their scepticism about the Shannon not running through that county geography is hopelessly against them.

MUNNIX [*viciously*] I don't care whether they come from Cork or from Tambuctoo. It's the berd—

GUNN [*amiably*] Now, Mr. Munnix, it really is desirable that we should have this little matter finally elucidated before we proceed with renewed vigour on the plane of the tin-tacks. So now, my good people you will, perhaps, be able to furnish me with the name of the town or village within the radius of which you projected your benign existence whilst sojourning on the banks of the Jordan—I mean, of course, the Shannon.

MRS. HANRAHAN [*pensively*] What in the name of goodness was it called then?

MICHAEL Well I'm blowed if I can think of it, though it's in my head.

MAURICE 'Tis in my head too, Michael Hanrahan, but all the same, I can't think of it.

MRS. HANRAHAN [*reminiscently*] It began with a Shan, too.

GUNN [*laughing, blithely*] Ha! Ha! Ha! the Bells of Shandon that sung so grand on—no, not on the Shannon, so it can't be Shandon.

MRS. HANRAHAN Begob I have it, sir, Shanagolden, taycher.

HANRAHAN [*jumping up excitedly*] Shanagolden, taycher, Shanagolden. Ah, I could swear all the books in Ireland that was the name of it. [*sonorously*] Shanagolden! Wan Moore made a song about it sir, but I'm no good at versifying and only bits of it come back to me. What is this it was then? Yes, this is how it went—Sweet Shanagolden, fare thee well [*sitting back on armchair, stroking beard, pensively trying to recall words of song*] Sweet Shanagolden, fare thee well.

MAURICE [*emotionally*] True for you Michael Hanrahan, Sweet Shanagolden fare thee well.

MICHAEL [*jumping up again*] Well, I remember now in going into the town there was won Haley a publican on one side with 'Guinness is good for you' in his window and opposite was another publican called Faley with a pecthur of a jolly red-faced ould man no berd on him at all but some little affair near his air, a glass on a table fornenst him and he saying to himself 'I prefer a Bass'.

MAURICE [*jumping up with excitement*] True for you, Michael Hanrahan, and now it comes before me as large as life, the pecthur of the jolly ould fellow with the little thing near his air and he saying to himself 'I Prefer a Bass'. Ah, but 'tis well you have described him. [*enthusiastically*] Upon my soul, Michael Hanrahan, you are great.

ROCHE [*losing patience with* MAURICE] And what are you yourself but a rib of your old brother's father christmas whiskers.

MICHAEL Indeed it's the tough whiskers has himself all his own and stiffer than mine.

MAURICE True for you, Michael Hanrahan, it is all that.

MICHAEL He shaves the chin, but that was out of a little vanity in the day of his youth and it's only a habit with him now.

ROCHE [*to* MICHAEL] The next thing you'll be telling maybe is that he used to court and was a soart of a Don June. If you do I'll faint.

GUNN [*to* ROCHE] You might even collapse like the sleuth in *Les Miserables*, when he made what was to him an astounding discovery that a criminal may also be a human being—oh, be careful, my young friend, do be careful.

MICHAEL [*jovially*] Morisheen was no law-dee-da, sir, but he got a bad fit wanst about a woman he seen in a train in Listowel, bought a ticket and went as far as Ballingrane with her. 'Twas her buzzum that enticed Morisheen.

MRS. HANRAHAN [*to* GUNN, *conversationally and confidentially*] Her bussum, sir. She was at some refection—

GUNN —at some reception—

MRS. HANRAHAN —at some perception and wearing one of them low neck dresses, and when Morisheen saw her she was leaning out the window and her buzzum heaving. Morisheen being young and innocent had no partiality—no par—par—

GUNN —no perspicacity, Mrs. Hanrahan, perhaps.

MRS. HANRAHAN —no perspikagity, thought she was a girl, but indeed what was she but a well-married woman.

MICHAEL What, married! She had eight or nine children already and Morisheen got the surprise of his life when he seen the husband

and troups come to meet her at Ballingrane. 'Why didn't you tell me that you had a husband and that he had eight children', sez Morisheen. 'How do you know they are his?' sez she and she laughing. She was a jolly sort of woman, sir, and she was only codding Morisheen.

MAURICE [*sadly*] True for you, Michael Hanrahan, she was codding me all the way from Listowel to Ballingrane.

MUNNIX [*suddenly breaking away from* MRS. MUNNIX *and making steps towards* GUNN] Where are we or where are we at all, taycher. Have we got into a despatch?

GUNN [*smilingly*] As a matter of fact it does seem we have got into an impasse.

MUNNIX Let it be a pass or a patch, look at ould Hanrahan laughing at us and let him be a Corkman or no, its wid the dint of roguery he's laughing.

GUNN [*with assumed severity to* HANRAHAN] Yes, Mr. Hanrahan, I now note you are shaking from a more or less suppressed access of risibility, but however subdued or concealed, your whole deportment shows the pleasure you are deriving from it.

MICHAEL It is because of ould Munnix reminding me of an ould soper I met with above in the City of Cork, sir. We'll have to get out sez I—we were in a bar—it's a half an hour gone the time by that clock—if that clock is right sez I. If it was right the nigger would have no right to be here sez he. I made a remark about something else and sez he, 'Where e'er you be', sez he, 'let the monsoon go free for the keeping of a hurrigane was the killing of me'. But of course ould sopers' talk is no converse for babies or ladies.

MAURICE True for you Michael Hanrahan, ould sopers talk is no talk for babies or ladies.

MUNNIX Off they go at gadgets the taycher after them [*to* GUNN] and what was the good of your having everything off tip-tap, tap-tip pit-pat if you can't stop them.

GUNN That's one of the psychological problems we have to deal with Mr. Munnix, the Hanrahan tendency to go off at tangents.

MUNNIX [*snappishly*] Gadgets gudgets, tadgets—what we have to deal with is the question of the kid pro cod, and to prove delibert villainy to them by means of the kicking horse and the cow with the blind eye.

GUNN [*blandly*] Well, I think the question of the *quid pro quo* has been satisfactorily disposed of from one point of view. I am coming to the other matters. And I observe that Mr. Hanrahan has ceased to chuckle.

MUNNIX [*gleefully*] The guilty conscience has frozen him.

GUNN I agree with Mr. Munnix, Mr. Hanrahan. Even without spectacles I can perceive that the whole surface of your expansive frontispiece both vertically, horizontally and peripherially betrays newly-awakened tremors of reminiscent culpability destroying with one fell blow all long-held credence in what might be termed your almost infallible content of simplicity and innocence. But hasn't Ezekiol said, 'Let the wicked man turn from his wickedness and live'. And we humbly await your contrite explanation of the reasons which prompted you to sell me a kicking horse, and the pro-Civil Bill Officer the cow with the blind eye.

MAURICE Well, sir, 'twas I sold the process-server the cow with the blind eye.

ROCHE [*rancously*] So 'twas you, me ould Don June, that sold me the cow with the blind eye, was it?

MUNNIX [*harshly to* ROCHE] Don't you be dishing off now or they'll be dishing off after you.

MICHAEL [*blandly*] A cow with a blind eye is as good as any other cow, and indeed, an', 'tisn't Morisheen you would expect to go belling around the fair that his baisht needed a coptician.

GUNN Well, no, certainly not—but the point is—

MUNNIX —the point is roguery and why not say it, taycher. Wasn't it roguery we had in our pit-pat, tip-tap, tap-tip.

GUNN The point is, Mr. Hanrahan, whether the transactions were not of a deliberate nature rather than an accidental one arising out of the simplicity and ingeniousness hitherto attributed to you and yours. In fact, Mr. Munnix, would go so far as to state that the simplicity was altogether on our side allowing us, vulgarly speaking, to be had by our childish belief in the naivety of others, myself in particular, Mr. Hanrahan, when I paid you a very good price for the kicking horse.

MICHAEL He usn't kick when I had him, sir.

GUNN But we have been informed by the man from Abbeyfeale that you had a method of dealing with that horse, Mr. Hanrahan, such as tinkers employ in dealing with donkeys and also in manoeuvring unruly equines.

MICHAEL [*blandly*] All lies, sir. The horse must have taken some fit when he left me. Anyway, sir, didn't you yourself say sell the horse to the Secondary taycher, Mr. O'Looney.

GUNN In accordance with the usual morality prevailing at horse fairs, Mr. Hanrahan, which is quite beside the issue raised between yourself and Mr. Munnix.

MICHAEL [*persisting*] The horse wasn't kicking when I had him, sir, but he was kicking with you and you sold him to Mr. O'Looney.

GUNN [*snappishly*] A man with a name like that was simply asking for it anyway. That might not be a quite satsifactory rejoinder to your riposte, Mr. Hanrahan, but I would have a better one if I really did mean to get my own back on the fellow in that way for the humiliating position in which that supercilious person once landed me in presence of the reverend manager of the school and of an individual whom I have elsewhere referred to as the Grand Cham of Tartary, by asking me the absurd conundrum as to what was the difference between a good old man, a bad old man and a clean old man.

MICHAEL [*laughing loudly and vacantly*] Faith, that was a stiff one, sir.

GUNN [*intensely*] You laugh and rightly so, Mr. Hanrahan, and that is what I also should have done and treated the creature's inane and vulgar impudence with the sneering contempt it deserved. Instead, I fell into the trap and got both indignant and insulted on the spot. 'There is very little difference, Mr. O'Looney', I said 'between a good old man and a bad old man if you view the matter', I said, 'from a certain angle. For example', I said 'an alleged bad old man being in the habit of letting off steam, might be less of a danger to Society than an alleged good old man, especially if the latter happened to contract Bright's disease of the kidneys. And, astounding as it may appear to the uninitiated Mr. O'Looney, it is quite possible that an individual may be, at one and the same time a good old man, a bad old man, and a clean old man'.

MICHAEL [*puzzled*] And did that bate him, sir?

GUNN [*ignoring interruption, continuing*] This gave the Grand Cham his chance. 'I really don't think, Mr. Jaymary Gunn', he said with an old smile and a grin, 'that your remarks are quite orthodox. Of course that sort of thing would be all right if you were addressing professors of medical jurisprudence, but there are ignorant people as well as children listening'. Then he gave a sly look at the reverend manager into whose green-grey eye there came a shade of blue. Not indigo blue, prussian blue, sky-blue or even navy blue, but china blue, that is, if china blue is the blue one sees on a genuine old willow pattern plate. And he gave a little glance at me over his glasses, that was all. But I knew from sorry experience that the more sedate he was the more dangerous.

MRS. MUNNIX [*darkly*] Hush, hush, taycher.

ROCHE Mrs. Munnix, you have a heart as well as a head and I praise you for it. [*to* GUNN] Mrs. Munnix is right—hush, hush, taycher.

MUNNIX [*rancously*] Hush, hush, hish-hish, hash-hash—what I want to know is what has happened to our tip-top, tap-tip, tip-tap.

ROCHE [*gaily*] Its gone colly west if you ask me.

MUNNIX [*angrily to* GUNN] You haven't even yet given him the presume.

GUNN The resumé?

MUNNIX The resoom of all the benefits the villain has from me— a fine farm with rent rates and taxes all fully paid and stocked with the best of cattle. Sixteen good cows, six dry heifers, two thundering brood mares, a new common car and a pony and trap for the young couple to take a gallivant in when they'd feel so disposed. A topping hay-shed and a first-class dwelling-house—exquisator—ially— exqueesat—

GUNN Exquisitely.

MUNNIX —exquisitely furnished. The room above the kitchen is fit for the Prince of Wales to walk into with a lovely round table with a shine on it and six dandy upblasted—upblistered—

GUNN —upholstered.

MUNNIX —upholstered chairs with beauteous expensive things on them that the wife calls anti-maccrackers.

MRS. MUNNIX Anti-macjaspers, Theobald.

GUNN Or, anti-maccassars, Mr. Munnix.

MRS. MUNNIX [*sweetly but definitely*] No taycher, anti-macjaspers.

GUNN [*evenly*] I stand corrected. After all ladies know more about the proper names of house articles than men do.

MRS. MUNNIX [*very pleased, smiling*] Thank you, taycher.

MUNNIX [*almost threateningly to* GUNN] Well, what are you doing now?

GUNN As a matter of fact, I am trying to recover my self-possession.

MUNNIX [*drily*] Well, while you are recovering, I'll tackle old beardy-puss myself and put a straight dishconnayre—bestgobare—

GUNN —Questionnaire.

MUNNIX —bestgobare will do me—I'm in no humour for fancy pronouncing. And I put to you a straight bestgobare, Michael Hanrahan, which is, will you or will you not pay me a thousand pounds for the loss of your daughter's whole leg—I'm leaving out the trimmings, I mean the hair and the teeth?

MICHAEL And I am telling you they were the expensive affairs, but it was the leg cost the big money entirely made special in France. Indeed me darlin' daughter has a gorgeous leg that she can hobble about in fine.

MUNNIX [*sneeringly*] Hobble about! A nice how-dee-do for a farmer's wife, hobble about!

MICHAEL [*suavely*] Ould Moll in the Wad used to say—and she was the shrewd dame—that the worst way in the world for a farmer's wife was to be tearing around slashin' and slavin', batin' the servant girls, getting wrinkles on her face and grey hair on her head from the dint of temper and parspiration, instead of sitting down on her cheer for herself, keeping an eye cocked and giving an order where suitable.

MAURICE [*enthusiastically*] True for you, Michael Hanrahan. Sound to you my bully man but it's fine you're talking.

MUNNIX The fact is, taycher, out pat-pit, tip-tap, tap-tip is now indeed finished so I'll have to give him off my own hat—

GUNN —off your own bat—

MUNNIX —a bultimatum and a final one.

GUNN An ultimatum! Oh, that's very serious, Mr. Munnix.

MUNNIX An ultimatum or a bultimatum, that's what I am now going to give you Michael Hanrahan—vig—vid—viv—

GUNN Viz.

MUNNIX Viz: that if you don't give me on the spot a thousand pounds parling—perling—

GUNN —sterling.

MUNNIX —a thousand pounds sterling, that daughter of yours that you see there fornenst you will be thrun to you in a heap in the corner.

MICHAEL [*blandly*] Indeed, it isn't in a broom or a motor car you have brought her back to me as it is. Indeed, its the most disrespectful way I ever seen a female woman treated since the day I was borned.

MAURICE True for you, Michael Hanrahan, you never seen such disrespect.

MRS. HANRAHAN Faith, 'tisn't too young I am either, and I never seen the likes no less. No wonder, my poor girl you'd be shaking from top to toe.

LENA [*drily*] *Si, si*, maman, but it isn't from laughter or from the ague I am shaking either [*shrugging shoulders indifferently*] *Mais qu'est-ce que vous voulez, c'est la guerre.*

MICHAEL [*enthusiastically*] Isn't she marvellous taycher, takes after her aunt Delia Daly that was noted through the County Cork for her larnin'. Delia was a holy show, sir, she was a fright. She could add up sums and add them down; she could carry them away in her head an subamash them and divilize them, she could. Reports were going that she could do a thing that no man ever was able to do since Arishtotle. Upon my soul sir, 'twas commonly reported she could do the rule of tray. And she told us there was a saying among the angident Irish—

GUNN —the ancient Irish—

MICHAEL [*continuing, oblivious of the interposition*] or among the angident English, I forget which, that a wig was as good as a wag or something like that. Lena is as quick as her, the Irish comes out of her as glib as the English or French.

GUNN [*slyly*] It certainly came out very quickly, Mr. Hanrahan, whichever it was.

MUNNIX [*savagely*] And I'll be as quick as her a daughter of a rogue and a rogue herself and they are all rogues. [*loudly*] I'll be as quick as her, and I am now going to catch her and throw her in a heap, and I don't care whether she breaks her wooden leg or not.

MRS. MUNNIX [*catching* MUNNIX *as he makes dart towards* LENA] Theobald be quiet. Theobald recollect you were called after Father Mathew. [*to* GUNN] That's what the doctor told me to say to him, taycher, when he'd get excited, upsetting that blood-pressure.

GUNN I am glad the plan is working, though he still looks dangerous. It is a mistake, Mr. Munnix, going to extremes, not to mention that physical gestures of this type was not provided for in our pit-pat arrangement. Nothing in excess, said a wise old Greek long ago, and this applies to temper as well as to drink.

MUNNIX [*stuttering*] Dud-ud-ud-ud-dud-

MRS. MUNNIX [*loudly*] Theobald recollect you were called after Father Mathew. Getting boliv is the worst thing for him, taycher. The doctor told us look out for hawks when he'd get boliv.

GUNN Stuttering is certainly a very ominous sign under such conditions. So try and control it, Mr. Munnix, or else look out for squalls.

MRS. MUNNIX [*somewhat sharply*] 'Twasn't stuttering the doctor named it at all, sir, but boliv the same as myself. And indeed, 'tisn't likely a professional gintleman like him would say boliv, if it wasn't a good English word.

GUNN Something to be said for your view ma'am, nevertheless, I doubt if boliv is to be found in the Oxford dictionary. Again, professional gentlemen are frequently good business men and are quite capable, if occasion requires of assuming a posture of humility. Miss Braddon's doctor, by the way, who had achieved an excellent bed-side manner, was also cute enough to dress for the part especially when attending to ladies.

PETE [*who for some time has been whispering in aside with* LENA *with some tickling, little giggles, etc., suddenly and aimlessly*] Theobald recollect you were called after Father Mathew!

ROCHE [*jocosely*] Ha! ha! Pete.

MRS. MUNNIX Is the boy gone crazy entirely or what is up with him, then?

PETE It's talking without thinking I was ma, but the taycher will understand, when I tell him I have got another dart from the eye of cupidity and I have fallen in love with Lena again.

MUNNIX [*making dart at* PETE *but is held back by* MRS. MUNNIX] Out, you colliflogical idiot, out!

LENA [*sweetly*] I have always been in love Pete, I have never changed. You remind me of the little song I sang for you once:

> *L'amour c'est le bonheur,*
> Oh, come and tease me;
> *L'amour c'est le bonheur,*
> Oh, come and squeeze me—
> *L'amour c'est le bonheur!*

PETE That's not the song we heard in the wireless though and sang together in the garden. And why shouldn't we sing it again.

LENA [*gleefully*] *Tres biens*, Pete.

[*They sing 'Sweetheart'. At beginning of last verse* PETE'S *mind wanders and looking recently upwards starts 'Mary, Mary quite contrary, how does—' when* LENA *grasps him vigorously by arm and they both finish the song with verve and gusto*]

MUNNIX [*breaking away from* MRS. MUNNIX, *to* PETE *furiously*] You fool, you booby, you non-con—you nan-con—you nin-con [*eying* GUNN] Which?

GUNN [*indifferently*] Presumably, nincompoop.

MUNNIX You nincompoop, get out of here.

PETE O.K. father. [*goes towards door with* LENA]

LENA [*looking back, archly*] O.K. fathers. Okee duck, too lee moand—

MUNNIX [*fiercely*] After all our trouble not a farthing benefit by it. And that fool of a son of mine in the finish to go and put the tin-pot on it. [*drily to* GUNN] You were going to say something there?

GUNN [*nonchalantly*] Oh, nothing much. But I have heard of the expression—a tin hat.

MUNNIX [*darkly*] As if it mattered whether it was a tin hat or a tin pot, he put on it when he done the harm. [*to* MRS. MUNNIX] Let us be going home. I wisht to God I was dead.

MRS. MUNNIX [*soothingly taking him by arm as they go towards door*] Don't be taking it too tragic, Theobald. They'll have childre with the help of God and they might turn out better than what we think.

MUNNIX Let us be hoping it, let us be hoping it. But it is a bitter thing to think that we were boozlebammed—

GUNN —bamboozled.

MUNNIX [*after short reflection, generously*] That's right, taycher, bambleboozed. It's better think we were bambleboozed by the ould man with the berd. [*they exit*]

ROCHE Well, whether we are boozlebammed or bambleboozed or—

GUNN or bamboozled.

ROCHE —or bamboozled; as we have no more to do, it seems to me we had better slack off.

GUNN Pack off, yes. We are now *de trop*. We have no longer any *raison d'etre* in these premises. Consequently, it's suitable and proper that we should make our evanishment with celerity. [*turning towards* HANRAHANS] Well, good afternoon lady and gentlemen.

ROCHE [*as they are going out*] It strikes me, taycher, that you have put them into a state of bustlement by what you said last.

GUNN Into a state of puzzlement? I don't see why saying 'good afternoon' should have that effect but they certainly seem nonplussed.

[ROCHE *and* GUNN *go out chortling. Pause.* MICHAEL *takes pipe from mouth and seems to be thinking hard.* MRS. HANRAHAN *and* MAURICE *follow suit.* MICHAEL *spits at mirror followed by* MAURICE, *whose spit goes lower.* MRS. HANRAHAN *makes an effort, spits, and goes higher than either.*]

MICHAEL [*suddenly*] I declare to my God but them taychers are getting madder every week. Doon-boon-soon good what did he say then.

MRS. HANRAHAN 'Twas noon, he said, Michael. I had a place with a faymale taycher long before I married you, and I recollect well she used to call the middle of the day, noon.

MICHAEL [*vigorously*] I declare to my God but them taychers haven't a splink at all, at all. Good after twelve o'clock [*sitting back on chair with deep sardonic laugh*] Good after twelve o'clock.

ALL THREE [*swaying backwards and forward and screaming with laughter*] Good after twelve o'clock! Good after twelve o'clock.

CURTAIN

The Coming of Ewn Andzale

IN ONE ACT

First printed in THE DUBLIN MAGAZINE (New Series Vol XXX
No 3) July–September 1954

CHARACTERS

CAPT. JAMES DAVENPORT,
DYMPHNA, *his wife*
QUEENIE ⎫
CISSIE ⎭ *their daughters*
POPHAM, *their son*
UNCLE SILAS
BRIDGET, *a servant*

PLACE

The Davenport's drawing room

TIME

The present

The Coming of Ewn Andzale

The scene takes place in the Davenport's drawing-room. In centre of room is an ottoman, to left of which is a small, oblong card-table. Near this a gramophone. To right of ottoman, a chair. At extreme right, at wall, is an upright piano with chair near it. To right of piano a door and to right of door a small sofa. Books are seen on the card-table. At rise of curtain, Captain Davenport is seen sitting on ottoman at right and Popham on left. Cissie is on chair at right of ottoman and Mrs. Davenport is on chair near piano but is facing auditorium, her left arm on back of chair.

DAVENPORT [*looking at watch*] Only half an hour to go, fancy. Still I wish Ewn Andzale had arrived. I feel on tenterhooks, somehow. I do wish the man came.

MRS. DAVENPORT Isn't the suspense agonising. No wonder, for, of course, if this piece of good luck hadn't come to us I don't know what would have happened to us, really.

DAVENPORT [*looking out window*] Queenie is coming up the path. She doesn't worry. In fact, I think she is quite sceptical about the whole thing.

POPHAM She is so learned or thinks she is that she doesn't believe in anything. I'm getting fed up though with the way she is going for me lately.

DAVENPORT You should make allowances, my boy, for what we used call in my young days a blue stocking. Then of course she is getting near thirty and no proposals. She is three years older than Cissie, isn't she?

CISSIE [*promptly*] Four years older than I papa.

MRS. DAVENPORT Girls in Ireland, young or old, and no matter how beautiful they may be, have no chance of getting married nowadays unless they have money. [*drearily*] Things have come to an awful pass.

POPHAM But things will be all right, mum, won't they when Ewn Andzale turns up. Hasn't he said he will give twenty thousand pounds each to Queenie and Cissie and will finance me in the starting of the garage. And, of course, he'll make everything chin-chin for yourself and father.

MRS. DAVENPORT [*somewhat hysterically*] Yes, of course he'll make everything chin-chin as you put it, for all of us. And, what nice things he said in his letter about the downfall of a good old Anglo-Irish family, our beautiful country residence burnt down by the Sinn Feiners and now reduced to pinching and scraping in this little suburban house in Monkstown driven even to the deplorable extreme of having to take in those bed-and-breakfast people. I never read such a sympathetic letter before. Oh he'll surely come at the very moment he said he would.

[*enter* QUEENIE]

QUEENIE [*sitting on sofa, drily*] You all seem to be in a state of tension. 'Pon my word you do look funny. Although, indeed, the whole affair is really more tragic than comic.

POPHAM Listen to her, dad! The silly old curlew, what is she sniggering about, anyway.

DAVENPORT [*wagging finger reprovingly*] Pop! Pop!

QUEENIE [*to* DAVENPORT] Oh, I don't mind poor half-baked Pop. He is most amusing really, every time he opens his mouth. A scream in fact. Notwithstanding his age, he is as excruciatingly Victorian as our furniture. Excruciating is the word. In passing him the other day when he was speaking to his pals, I heard him refer to the girls he hob-nobs with in Grafton Street as 'tarts'.

DAVENPORT [*sternly*] Now, Queenie, Queenie. But what's wrong? Have you heard something about Ewn Andzale not turning up to-night or what?

QUEENIE No, papa, I've heard nothing whatever about the thing.

DAVENPORT About the thing! One would imagine by the way you talk that you didn't give a fig whether the man came or not.

MRS. DAVENPORT [*appealingly*] But, Queenie, why should you be that way? Oughtn't you be as glad as anyone of us for the deliverance Ewn Andzale has promised us.

DAVENPORT [*significantly*] In fact, I think she should be a little more glad if anything than anybody else.

QUEENIE [*drily*] Your hint is not thrown away, papa. I can assure you, however, that I am not in the least unaware of or indifferent to the depredations of anno domini.

DAVENPORT   Well then, what were you hinting at? I suppose you were hinting at something, weren't you?

QUEENIE   As well as the rest of you, I have read that letter to mother from an individual signing himself, herself, or itself, Ewn Andzale. At first, I said to myself this is really too good to be true and then I began to reflect on the origin of the so-called fairy tales.

DAVENPORT   [drily] Oh, really!

POPHAM   [scoffingly] Huh! Huh!

QUEENIE   [blandly] I mean those tales conceived ages ago when the world was young, and the authorship of which is unknown.

POPHAM   Good God, Governor what do you make of her?

DAVENPORT   I don't know what to make of her, but let her dish it out whatever it is, it might do her good.

QUEENIE   [suavely] The motive or aspiration in every one of those fairy tales is the very same as that behind the wording of this letter from Ewn Andzale—namely, a wish to by-pass by some fluke or other the intolerable and seemingly unjust workings of fate. The wish in the fairy tales represented an emanation from the subconscious self which is also the case in this letter from Ewn Andzale, except that I believe that the whole thing as far as the latter composition is concerned, was done almost entirely unconsciously.

DAVENPORT   [gruffly] What nonsense! Do you mean to say that Ewn Andzale was unconscious when he wrote that letter to your mother.

POPHAM   [in a ribald way] Daft! Those whom God—those whom the gods wish to employ—to deploy—to—to—to—

DAVENPORT   Those whom the Gods wish to destroy they first drive mad.

QUEENIE   [indifferently] You have got him out of it all right, papa. This attitude, however, doesn't get me any further. I should say nothing more I suppose—I should let you carry on but then I have to consider that the shock to mother in her present mental condition may have serious consequences when this Ewn Andzale fails to keep his appointment. [to MRS. DAVENPORT] I was hoping mother, ever since the letter came, that sooner or later some little glimmer would dawn on you respecting the actualities of the situation.

MRS. DAVENPORT   [tensely] What under heaven are you driving at and [sharply] pray what do you mean by my mental condition, Queenie Davenport?

QUEENIE Your mental condition mama—and now I hope in giving you a little shock that it will save you from a greater one—namely that your mental condition was not at all what it should have been when you wrote that letter to yourself and signed it Ewn Andzale. You were in exactly the same frame of mind as those old authors of the fairy tales except that, as I have already stated, you were probably quite unaware of what you were doing when you penned the thing.

DAVENPORT 'Pon my honour I never heard such nonsense in my life before. [*lightly*] Mrs. Davenport, you haven't gone suddenly crazy, have you?

MRS. DAVENPORT Not that I know of, James. I can't understand what object the dreadful girl has in going on in this way.

CISSIE It's you that's going mad, Queenie, not mother. Pop might have been a bit rude when he said you were daft, but—

DAVENPORT I do hope, Queenie, you don't talk in that strain to others. It wouldn't do you any benefit.

POPHAM I bet she does, dad. That's why she never got married perhaps. A fellow would be afraid to marry a girl, who gave out old guff like that.

QUEENIE [*sweetly, to* POPHAM] Who are you speaking for Pop, the nincompoops? Mother says our single blessedness is due to lack of the rhino leaving charming little Cissie stranded as well as me. But, whatever is the cause, having two unmarried daughters on her hands has had a good deal to do with the derangement that has taken place in Mama's nerve centres. But Pop there, the incomparable Pop, is the chief cause of the crisis which has overtaken her.

POPHAM [*suddenly and loudly*] You're a liar!

DAVENPORT [*severely*] Now Pop, this won't do, it won't do at all.

POPHAM I apologise. But she'd make a fellow swear his head off.

QUEENIE Swear his head off? Well now, what a funny thing to say. Nevertheless, mother, I am afraid Pop is the chief causative factor in putting you into that frame of mind which eventually egged you to write that letter to yourself. Didn't you work heaven and earth to get him something to do in order to keep him at home, finally, in desperation getting him that job in the garage and excusing yourself by citing the cases of Russian Grand Dukes who drove cabs in Paris after the first great war.

MRS. DAVENPORT [*weakly*] Pop always liked machines.

POPHAM Of course I did, mother, and I know all about gadgets and things. I often told you I'd love to have a garage, and I wouldn't have lost that job but for the row I had with that darned fool of a proprietor.

MRS. DAVENPORT Oh, that horrid dreadful man. Only for him you would never have ever thought of going to British Columbia.

QUEENIE And that's what brought the world crashing about poor mama's ears—Pop leaving his job and going to British Columbia.

MRS. DAVENPORT [*fearfully*] What wonder and he my only son.

QUEENIE No wonder about it, but if your mental balance had been stronger the worry would not have caused such a brainstorm resulting in the bizarre development of your writing a letter to yourself. Otherwise, you would probably have effected an endo-psychic transfer, that is you would have driven the trouble from your brain down into your breadbasket, with, very likely, nothing more serious accruing therefrom than a severe, but temporary, attack of gastritis.

DAVENPORT I have already told you, Queenie, that I have never heard such nonsense in my life before as that I have been hearing from you today, and now I tell it to you again. Even if Ewn Andzale doesn't turn up to-night, that wouldn't prove that your mother, Mrs. Davenport, did such an outlandish and nonsensical thing as to write a letter to herself.

POPHAM [*enthusiastically*] Of course, it wouldn't. Stout fellow Governor, good egg.

DAVENPORT Again, even if there was anything in this endo-endo-whiskers stuff, will you kindly explain by what course of reasoning you have arrived at the conclusion that your mother is a weak-minded person or what evidence you can bring forward to justify you in making such a statement. My experience is that she is the opposite [*laughing*] in fact a little too much so sometimes for my taste.

QUEENIE You are mistaking bouts of obstinacy for strongmindedness, papa. You have forgotten or perhaps you never knew, and perhaps she never told you, that several of her nearest relatives were, at any rate, partially, sub-normal. But I recollect, when a child, hearing her tell Lady Scrimgeour that with the exception of her Cockney half-brother, Silas, all the rest of her brothers and sisters were a little bit off the top.

MRS. DAVENPORT [*determinedly and harshly*] It is absolutely false, Queenie. I may have regretted my brothers' way of life. They believed in a short life and a merry one. 'Let us eat, drink and be merry'—that was their motto, having no urge, as they used to put it, to be continually trying to keep themselves fit in order to qualify eventually for a sojourn in the condemned cell of old age and, of course, the poor chaps did die rather young. But that didn't mean that they were mentally defective, and I deny utterly that I ever said a horrid thing about my late brothers as that they were a little bit off the top.

QUEENIE I daresay you expressed yourself more elegantly my dear, even though what you did say, if my memory isn't playing pranks with me, amounted to the same thing. Having relieved yourself to Lady Scrimgeour, you probably magaged to forget all about the unpleasant subject by the simple and usual process of stowing away all thoughts of it in the recesses of your sub-consciousness.

MRS. DAVENPORT [*darkly*] Shu!

QUEENIE Please, mother, don't look at me like that as if you were taking me for a murderess. As I said, I am doing all this for your own good. No necessity to take certain family defects too tragically either. There are several families throughout the country of light textured minds whom the Irish peasantry term 'airy', but who rarely become inmates of lunatic asylums. Some of my uncles— your brothers—could possibly be described as border-line cases, [*laughs*] somewhat like Pop for example.

POPHAM [*with assumption of some dignity*] Well, you're gone beyond the borderline, anyway, Queenie, and dad thinks the same as I do.

CISSIE [*laughing*] As Pop himself would put it, he has given you one in the kisser this time, Queenie, but neatly and in a gentlemanly way.

QUEENIE [*shrugging shoulders, indifferently*] I can take it.

DAVENPORT You certainly deserved it, Queenie, for your reference to Pop as a borderline case was hitting below the belt and besides was unjustified. He may not be able to pass exams, but he knows a whole lot about machines, and I don't know but he was better than yourself at one subject anyhow, namely Hydrostatics and Pneumatics. I have heard him talking to his pals about machinery, batteries and so forth and his remarks were succinct, sensible and to the point. I have no doubt if Ewn Andzale sets him up in a garage of his own, he will do finely thank you.

QUEENIE [*indifferently*] Shouldn't be surprised. However, it is with poor mom I am at present concerned with rather than Pop and [*to* MRS. DAVENPORT] I do wish you wouldn't be thinking I want to hurt your feelings for, after all, your relations are also mine. What I really would like you to do now is to try and bring back to your consciousness the circumstances in which took place the instinctive act of writing that letter.

MRS. DAVENPORT [*scornfully*] Try and recall the circumstances under which a thing didn't take place! You *would* have a right to say I was silly if I tried to do anything of the kind. [*bitterly*] I repeat I never wrote the letter. I don't care what you say about endo—endo—I never wrote that letter.

POPHAM Of course you didn't, mom. Didn't dad laugh at her endo-whiskers. We all know she's talking through her hat.

CISSIE [*decidedly*] I don't care what Queenie says. I am certain mom never wrote that letter.

DAVENPORT [*ditto*] Dymphna never could have written that letter, Queenie. She'd never keep on denying it so determinedly if she had. Even if she did it in a trance some inkling of it would have dawned on her.

QUEENIE [*drily*] Then who wrote the letter papa, if mom didn't?

DAVENPORT [*somewhat weakly*] Ewn Andzale, I presume.

QUEENIE I don't know whether any of you have noticed it that while this mythical Ewn Andzale for some mysterious reason headed the missive En Route, the postmark on the envelope is Bangor where mother was on holiday. Herself and the letter arrived practically together.

DAVENPORT [*offhandedly*] A mere coincidence I expect.

CISSIE Of course, a coincidence. The handwriting is quite different anyway, so what?

QUEENIE It is a bit different and yet—. I am not very well up in the psychology of the matter, but I think I read somewhere that persons in the state mother was in when she wrote the letter develop a faculty for doing things that they would be incapable of doing in their normal condition. In this way she managed to assume the caligraphy as well as the personality of the particular Father Christmas she had in mind. By the way she has quite a supply of the same kind of notepaper as that on which Father Christmas Ewn Andzale expressed himself.

CISSIE [*with the desperation of one fighting a loosing battle*] That's nothing. Anybody could write on that kind of notepaper. I saw quite a lot of it yesterday in Combridge's window.

MRS. DAVENPORT Of course you did Cissie. [*severely*] But do you know what it is, Queenie, I am now really beginning to look on you as a murderess. You must have some dreadful motive in trying to persuade me that I wrote a letter to myself.

QUEENIE [*laughing*] Honestly, mother, I feel like a murderess at the moment. Nevertheless, duty has to be done, and I must mention, in pursuance of further elucidating the matter, that one thing did puzzle me for a bit, namely, why you should have chosen such a weird and unconvincing cognomen as Ewn Andzale.

DAVENPORT Probably Scotch. They have some very outlandish names in Scotland.

POP [*wisely*] Haven't they MacEwn?

DAVENPORT [*promptly*] You are right my boy, they have.

QUEENIE And then I thought of mother's gallant if futile attempts to escape from reality by plunging herself into the diversion of trying to solve crossword puzzles.

DAVENPORT [*impatiently*] What under heaven are you trying to deduce from that? Everyone does crossword puzzles nowadays. Occasionally I have a go at one myself. A harmless amusemant.

QUEENIE [*blandly*] Certainly. Crossword puzzles, reading, etc., are very useful in making existence more pleasant and bearable as ancillaries to the main purpose in life with its various duties, social obligations and so on. But when crossword puzzles absorb all one's energies that is a sign of mental ill-health. Which is the case with mother.

MRS. DAVENPORT I did a share of them, that was all.

QUEENIE Oh, you did more than what I would call a share of them, mama. You bought the *Times* and the *Daily Telegraph* for the sole purpose of doing their crosswords, aslo the *Sunday Times* and the *Observer,* not to mention the books of crosswords you went through. You didn't content yourself with the simpler ones either, and but for its pathetic aspect, it would have been diverting considering your educational background, such as your indifferent grounding the Classics and your lack of a thorough knowledge of Greek and Roman mythology, your continued and desperate but invariably unavailing attempts to solve the Ximenes Crossword in the *Observer*.

And it was whilst reflecting on mama's crossword activities that I got on the explanation of that nondescript cognomen, Ewn Andzale.

POP [*laughing rudely*] Huh! Huh! Huh!

DAVENPORT [*amusedly*] Well, really Queenie, so you did, did you! And how?

QUEENIE Quite simple. Everyone knows that anagrams play a considerable part in the composition of crosswords. And having taken the name Ewn Andzale to pieces so to speak I discovered that it was a meaningless anagram of New Zealand, the country by the way, that vulgar Cockney half-brother emigrated to. So that it is clear that the deliverer is to arrive from that country, however peculiar it may seem that he should write from Bangor, County Down.

MRS. DAVENPORT [*tearfully*] You are all beginning to believe her. I feel that you are. She has convinced you.

DAVENPOST Not a bit of it, old girl. We were listening to her, that's all.

POPHAM You'll have the laugh at her mother, when Ewn Andzale turns up on the tide of the clock.

CISSIE You are right, Pop. We'll all have the laugh at Queenie, then.

DAVENPORT [*jocosely*] Yes, Queenie. We'll all have a laugh at you all right.

MRS. DAVENPORT [*bursting into tears*] He must come! If he doesn't, you will all think then that I did such a dreadful thing. What shall I do if he doesn't come. [*weeps again*].

POPHAM Of course, he'll come. It's a dead cert., so far as I'm concerned.

DAVENPORT Shame her by jove! It's nearly up to the time and I have a telepathic feeling that he is already near at hand.

POPHAM By gad, I feel that way, too, as if there was something in the air.

CISSIE [*to* MRS. DAVENPORT *who has recommenced to weep*] Don't mind Queenie's snorts, mother, Ewn Andzale will come.

DAVENPORT and POPHAM Ewn Andzale will come!

DAVENPORT Is that a step on the gravelled walk?

POPHAM I thought I heard something.

MRS. DAVENPORT [*pensively*] I am reminded somehow of the days that are gone when we were children and used put our ears to the

153

ground listening for the sound of the carriage bringing back our elders, when they were away all day on some excursion or other. We'd know the sound of our own carriage and pair. If you were in the country now, you couldn't hear the motor car. And even if you did, you wouldn't know one motor car from another. We had variety in those days. And people were individualities. Now, like motor cars, they are all machines.

POPHAM [*suddenly*] By jingo, that was a step.

DAVENPORT [*looking at wrist watch*] It's Ewn Andzale's hour. It Is exactly nine o'clock.

[*Except* QUEENIE, *they sit up straight and listen in tense fashion. Suddenly a loud peremptory knock is heard at the front door.*]

MRS. DAVENPORT [*jumping up and holding on to back of chair*] I hear Bridget walking. She is going to answer the knock. [*tensely*] Can it be he? Can it be he?

[BRIDGET *is heard opening the front door. Then follows a loud, penetrating, agonising scream. They all seem paralysed with fright. Eventually* QUEENIE *rises and goes towards door.*]

QUEENIE Somebody must do something when the brave young man of the family shirks it. [*half-turning to* POPHAM] Coward! Coward!

POPHAM You are shaking yourself with terror, and it's only out of cussedness you are doing anything. A man might face the lion's mouth and get the jitters from a dashed old scream like that.

[BRIDGET *suddenly opens door which she leaves ajar. She appears to be frantic with terror.*]

MRS. DAVENPORT [*agonisingly*] Bridget, Bridget, what was it and who was it?

BRIDGET I seen ne'er a wan, some brat I suppose that knocked and skedaddled, but a mouse ran up my leg and he's there ayet.

[*Shrieks from* MRS. DAVENPORT, QUEENIE *and* CISSIE]

BRIDGET He's down, now. There he is on the flure.

[CISSIE *jumps on chair,* MRS. DAVENPORT *scrambles up piano and* QUEENIE *gets on sofa.* POPHAM *bursts into unrestrained laughter pointing at* QUEENIE *standing on the sofa.*]

QUEENIE [*angrily to* POPHAM] You wretch, you wretch [*flings book at* POPHAM *who manages to catch hold of it; he clasps his knees doubles himself up and roars with laughter.*]

BRIDGET [*apparently enjoying the comic catastrophe*] It's all right now, misses and ma'am. He's gone the mouse. He eshcaped out the door.

[MRS. DAVENPORT *gets off piano, sits in armchair*]

QUEENIE [*getting off sofa, sneeringly to* POPHAM] So you would compare this natural reaction to your own arrant cowardice to your advantage. Without any scientific knowledge of humanity or of anything else, you are of course completely ignorant of the fact that there's a certain section of the female anatomy that is allergic to mice.

POPHAM [*in hollow tones*] Gosh, father!

DAVENPORT [*ditto*] Gosh!

MRS. DAVENPORT [*suddenly and unexpectedly taking advantage of the situation*] They're sterilised—I mean they are—

CISSIE [*intervening*] Paralysed?

MRS. DAVENPORT No, that's not the word either. They're—they're petrified. Yes that's it—petrified. All they can say is gosh! You awful girl. My God, if my poor mother had heard a thing like that! If she didn't die in a faint she would never have got over the shock of it.

QUEENIE You are making grandmother out to be a complete idiot. I admit you have some reason if it is true that she used drape the legs of our chaste Adam sideboard with its concave and convex panellings.

MRS. DAVENPORT [*sharply*] I admit she went a little too far there. But she was quite justified in covering the legs of our round mahogany dining table. They were—well they were what they were

QUEENIE [*slyly*] Nevertheless she has some little moral weaknesses, hadn't she? I heard she used say 'dang' and that her crony, Lady Scrimgeour, used swear like a trooper.

MRS. DAVENPORT [*decidedly*] Lady Scrimgeour used not! Ladies were allowed to say 'dang' in certain circumstances such as hitting one's toe against a stone, for instance, but only amongst themselves when men or children were not present.

QUEENIE She snuffed—grandmother I mean.

MRS. DAVENPORT [*in angry puzzlement*] Well, what about it, if she did, snuff is good fo sneezing.

QUEENIE [*blandly*] Whilst Lady Scrimgeour and Mrs. Gubkins smoked pipes of strong tobacco. The little window in the top back room where they used sequester themselves for the purpose was like a chimney on a summer's evening with puffs coming through it.

155

MRS. DAVANPORT [*lamely*] They both suffered from asthma, that's why.

POPHAM Don't mind her mum. She's only wagging a red legging in your eye.

DAVENPORT A red herring.

MRS. DAVENPORT So that's what she's at. [*grimly to* QUEENIE] But since you recollect so much about the red herrings—the dangs, snuffs and smokes, surely you haven't forgotten what happened to the young and beautiful if impecunious Jane Hewetson, and why.

QUEENIE Oh that was the lady wasn't it who shouted 'My God, what a fine pair of legs Captain Curling has got?' I suppose you would say in the lingo of the period that she was a bit fast.

MRS. DAVENPORT [*snappishly*] I don't know whether she was fast or not, but you know what happened to her for making that indecent remark, which by the way was not as indecent as the remark you made to Pop about— [*short pause*]. You know that the men, moreover the libertines among them, were more furious about it than the women, that nobody would marry her, beautiful and all as she was, and that she didn't properly resume her place in society till she was well over forty, when she came in for a large legacy and went churchy and was no longer a rival to the young girls in the marriage market.

QUEENIE [*languidly*] I believe I did hear about that then, but like Queen Victoria I was not greatly amused. [*Suddenly and gaily*]. But 'pon my honour, mother, you don't know how relieved I am at finding you possessing certain psychological reserves of strength which enable you to make a side-step so to speak when a calamitous disappointment overtakes you. Not so with Cissie, father and Pop. They certainly look petrified but, I am certain, not for the reason you have given. I have a hunch you have landed them in a worse condition than you are yourself. [*laughs blithely*]

MRS. DAVENPORT [*promptly*] Of course, I am disappointed and broken-hearted, but I have a ray of hope he will come yet.

POPHAM [*without conviction*] He may come to-morrow, if he doesn't come to-night.

DAVENPORT [*ditto*] There's absolutely no reason why he shouldn't come to-morrow if he doesn't come to-night. He may have missed his conveyance, train or boat or plane or whatever it may have been.

CISSIE [*ditto*] He might come to-night yet.

MRS. DAVENPORT [*tearfully*] Oh, you don't believe he will. You don't believe he will come at all. [*querulously to* BRIDGET] Please close that door, Bridget.

BRIDGET I forgot all about it with the hillabilloo, ma'am. And be the same token I believe I forgot also to— [*As* BRIDGET *moves to close door, a large, clean-shaven man wearing a stetson hat appears in the doorway*]

ALL [*including* BRIDGET *but excepting* QUEENIE] Ewn Andzale!

SILAS No, that's not my name. In the far-off days when I used those aitches, which I should not have used, and did not use those aitches, which I should have used, and there was no help in me, Dymphna used call me her vulgar cockney half-brother, Silas.

MRS. DAVENPORT Silas! Good gracious you can't be Silas, you're so different.

SILAS Tempora—tempora—

QUEENIE [*promptly*] *Tempora mutantur, nos et mutamur in illis.*

SILAS Thanks a lot, missie. Dymphna is still puzzled and suspicious, not knowing that I was associated with a couple of University men when I first went to New Zealand, which did the trick for me, and having a good ear for music I managed to achieve a magnificent Hoxford and Cambridge accent, unlike the Higginbotham family who hailed from Islington that a battleship wouldn't knock out of the habit of saying 'wiv' instead of with.

QUEENIE [*gaily*] You certainly are a smart guy, Uncle Silas.

SILAS [*ditto*] Guess I am, rather. And what fun I used have at the University chaps who went backwoods after having married poor Scotch and Cork girls, one of them rolling his 'r's' and t'other occasionally slipping out a 'dat' and even sometimes saying'butther'.

MRS. DAVENPORT [*severly*] Tragic rather than funny if you ask me. I know our own case since we lost caste. Of course, it was their own fault I suppose, but nevertheless, Silas, you should have been grateful to them for giving you the accent.

SILAS Oh, they didn't give it to me, I took it from them the same as you'd take mumps or measles. But it was gas, the amusing but not malicious exchanges that used often take place between us when we used meet in the vestibules of the good hotels.

MRS DAVENPORT [*showing a gleam of hope, half to herself*] In the vestibules of the good hotels? Well then, you did—by the way what were you doing in New Zealand, Silas?

SILAS [*as if trying to think*] What was I doing? Oh I was a bricklayer.

MRS. DAVENPORT [*disgustedly*] A bricklayer! A bricklayer staying in good hotels!

CISSIE New Zealand might be different in that way from here, mother.

MRS. DAVENPORT Perhaps. [*snappishly to Silas*] In any case what use would an accent be to a bricklayer, irrespective of whether he misused the aspirate or not which you do still by the way.

SILAS [*smiling*] Oh, I only do that sort of thing now for fun.

QUEENIE [*slyly*] I can see that, Uncle Silas.

SILAS [*taking letter from pocket*] Meanwhile I have something here that doesn't belong to me, I found it on the pavement and seeing your front door open—

BRIDGET [*interrupting*] The hillabilloo—

SILAS I walked right in to restore to you your property [*hands letter to* QUEENIE] It's addressed to Mrs. Davenport.

QUEENIE The letter from Ewn Andzale! Somebody—perhaps it was myself must have accidentally dropped it. I suppose you read it, Uncle Silas. You needn't excuse yourself. If you just glanced at it I am certain curiosity would force you to go the whole hog— *n'est-ce pas?*

SILAS [*quizzically*] *Oui-oui.* Its contents are certainly outside our ordinary experiences of life wherein, if you don't give, you won't get; like going in to a grocer's shop where what you buy is weighed out to you to a nicety, parcelled up and handed to you and that's that. And the principle is so universal and so exact that I often wondered whether electricity wasn't at the botom of it. Whereas this letter is something like what you'd get from Alice in Wonderland.

QUEENIE That was practically what I said Uncle, that it was of the fairy tale order and they all came down on me like a house of bricks making me out to be a criminal.

DAVENPORT Now, Queenie, that's not correct. What we objected to principally was your using the fairy tale stuff to incriminate your mother by charging her that she wrote the letter to herself.

SILAS [*gaily*] So you did that, Queenie. I now know your name is Queenie anyway. So you actually charged your mother with doing that.

QUEENIE I did.

SILAS Surprising if she did such a silly thing. In her young days anyhow, Dymphna was supposed to be the brainy member of her family. I never knew her to do anything odd or strange or foolish, except once when she rushed into the house in a state of great excitement saying she had seen a real satyr—not a goat she said—but a real satyr in the corner of the Big Shrubbery which, funnily enough was smaller in extent than the wood they called the Small Shrubbery, but the Big Shrubbery was on a slope was darkish and had a certain awesome appearance about it, and it was in the corner of the Big Shrubbery that she said she saw the satyr.

MRS. DAVENPORT [*deprecatingly*] Silas, please!—

SILAS It isn't fair I admit, for I can assure you Queenie, she didn't half get laughed at for her pains. And what was more humiliating, the humorous Dr. Forster who was present jokingly advised that she should give up learning Greek or it might cause a fissure in her brain pan.

QUEENIE [*significantly*] Ah!

MRS. DAVENPORT [*sharply and quickly*] What are you 'ah-ing', for. I was only fourteen years of age at the time, two years younger than Lucy Walker-Lee who was at the Alexandra with you, and 'twas you yourself told us how she saw the skeleton of a Dinosaur in the Bog of Allen, which turned out to be a huge piece of bog-oak.

SILAS [*to Queenie*] That's what you'd call a—a—

QUEENIE A *tu quoque.*

SILAS Oh Dymphna was always first-rate at that sort of thing in the gay old days at Tubrid House.

MRS. DAVENPORT [*stiffly*] I wouldn't exactly call them gay, Silas. We used go to the races, of course, like all the county people. In fact we were rather quiet folks, croquet, tennis, spoil five in the evenings, occasional dances and so on.

SILAS [*slyly*] And canoodling.

MRS. DAVENPORT I don't understand what you mean by canoodling. Everything was correct and nice with no vulgarity.

SILAS Quite so; nevertheless the young ladies knew how to fish notwithstanding their skirts went to the ground and all that. Which reminds me of the story a nursery maid told me of the clever manner in which you managed to land the Captain.

MRS. DAVENPORT [*rapidly*] Men were not so mercenary in those days.

159

12

DAVENPORT [*with pretended seriousness*] Silas, Silas, this is like telling tales out of school.

SILAS Shocking! However, I'd like to make things more lively as I have been unwittingly the cause of what I can now see was a tragic anti-climax for Dymphna in mistaking me for Ewn Andzale. [*lightly*] But don't they say half a loaf is better than no bread, and I am really not so poor, Dymphna, as perhaps I have led you to believe. I did bricklaying certainly, but later on I did some contracting.

MRS. DAVENPORT [*in pleased surprise*]: Contracting! Contractors make the world of money in Dublin.

SILAS And I also went wool-gathering.

POPHAM [*laughing loudly*] That's jolly good, Uncle Silas—it's jolly funny.

SILAS [*drily*] Oh is it! Nevertheless, young fellow, woolgathering in New Zealand doesn't mean day-dreaming, but is supposed to be a method of money-making.

MRS. DAVENPORT [*more pleased*] Money-making!

SILAS Money-making, yes. But it is difficult to understand how you can be so materialistic, Dymphna, and, apparently at the same time have become so evangelistic, that is if the titles of these books staring me in the face on the table mean anything. My God, what a selection!—Pearson on the *Creed*; Paley on the *Origins of Christianity*; Moscheim's *Ecclesiastical History*; Woods' *Natural History* —well that's dusty enough—but here we have again Taylor's *Holy Living and Dying*; Hooker's *Sermons*: Latimer's *Preparation for Communion*. Is this a Plymouth Brother establishment or what?

MRS. DAVENPORT Nonsense, Silas. Of course, we don't tell people about it, but we really keep those books on the table to give an air of respectability to the place. They were left to me by my cousin the rector, the Rev. Julian Goodlake, together with this house and all that Victorian furniture you see around you. Of course, nobody here reads those books except perhaps [*sarcastically*] our erudite Queenie.

QUEENIE Well, I suppose, I have to admit the soft impeachment, though my bent is really for modern science and philosophy and notwithstanding the fact that I am really allergic to—

MRS. DAVENPORT [*interrupting, harshly*] Please don't use that dreadful word again. I really must forbid you Queenie, to use that word again.

QUEENIE Mother, don't give yourself away like that. There is absolutely nothing wrong with the word *per se* whatever may have been wrong a short while ago with my application thereof.

SILAS [*slyly to Queenie*] Dymphna is getting her rag out so let us get back to—how is this the French are alleged to put it?

QUEENIE [*promptly*] *Retournon a nos moutons.*

SILAS Clever girl by gad! Yes, let us return to the money question. Well, my dear sister, I am really not badly off in the material way and being old and single, I took a hunch to leave New Zealand and return here in the hope of meeting a relation and perhaps finishing up here.

MRS. DAVENPORT [*cordially*] You could stay with us if that would suit, and then we needn't take in any more of those B and B people.

SILAS I'll consider over that. I'm not a Croesus like Ewn Andzale; nevertheless, Dymphna, I think I can do something substantial in the way outlined in the Josser's letter to yourself.

MRS. DAVENPORT [*somewhat hysterically and emitting a little chortle*] Thank you ever so much.

SILAS This doesn't mean, Queenie, any contradiction to your fairy tale theories nor to the deduction to be drawn from the little parable of the grocer's shop. For, when I was emigrating to New Zealand as poor as a church mouse, the Captain here acted handsomely by me.

DAVENPORT [*off-handedly*] Oh, I only did what any decent connection would have done in the cirs.—nothing extra.

MRS. DAVENPORT [*reminiscently*] Ah those good old days, you had plenty of money then, James. Would you ever have believed, Silas, that you'd see him as he is now, barely able to afford two new suits a year, for, with all our other misfortunes he lost nearly everything he had in the slump in the Marconi Shares.

QUEENIE [*suddenly rising from sofa, putting hand to mouth and emitting a little dry cough*] Well, now that everything is so dusty, I think the charge made against me of being a would-be murderess should be withdrawn—being so charged Uncle Silas, became by analysis and deduction or by synthesis and induction, I don't know which, I flatter myself that I proved up to the hilt that mother herself wrote that letter from Ewn Andzale. I have a hunch, Uncle Silas, that you also have guessed the secret, and since owing to the impingement of the events of this evening on her fore consciousness, I am certain she is now quite clear as to the cirs. in which the foul deed was committed, and I suggest, therefore, that she should make a full confession in the matter not merely because of my right to be cleared of matricidal intention, but also for the therapeutic purpose of cleansing her own mind of whatever traces of the obsession that may still be lingering there.

CISSIE [*brusquely*] Queenie give it a breeze! The whole pack of us are a selfish lot thinking all the time of ourselves and not saying a word of welcome to Uncle Silas. He doesn't even know my name yet.

MRS. DAVENPORT We are certainly most ill-mannered Cissie, but before doing the right thing by our guest, I must really first try to bring this obstreperous girl to her own senses, which is certainly more necessary than that she should bring me to mine, since you all know I am in full possession of them, thank goodness!

POPHAM Hear, hear, mum—that's the stuff to give her.

SILAS [*laughing, to* QUEENIE] If Dymphna is as good at repartee as she was in her young days when the girls were rivals for the eligible males who were sadly in a minority you are in for it, Queenie. They used all play tennis, and it was at a tennis tournament that she knocked out her redoubtable opponent, Florence Gabbett, not at the game by the way, but in a deadly verbal encounter.

MRS. DAVENPORT I had completely forgotten.

SILAS [*speaking to* QUEENIE *but not in an 'aside'*] So would I, very likely, have forgotten too but for the peculiarities of the encounter, between the pair gabbling at each other surrounded by a bevy of damsels calling each other 'love', 'dear', 'darling' and all that, so that being only then a kid and unversed in the devious ways of femininity I was nonplussed; till later on my eyes were opened when hearing some of Dymphna's faction screaming with delight, and gloating over the condition in which she left poor Florence, pale as a ghost, as they put it, and shaking like an aspen leaf.

MRS. DAVENPORT Alas, Silas, whatever talents I may have once possessed in that way are now but a memory. But even if I still had any such abilities, do you think I should be so hard-hearted as to use them for the purpose of humiliating or in any was giving pain to my beloved daughter, no matter what unpleasantness she may cause me by insisting that I wrote the Andzale letter. Oh no, if I succeed in bringing her to her senses it will be in a christian and motherly way, Silas.

CISSIE You're as bad as Queenie to worry either, mother. If Ewn Andzale never comes, and I for one don't care a fig now whether he does or not, I suggest that we should all come to the rational conclusion that somebody wrote the letter out of a hoax.

MRS. DAVENPORT Very nice of you Cissie, but I won't even adopt that for a defence; in fact I am not going to make any defence at all since there is nothing for me to defend in any baseless charge which may be made against me. I am only going to make a simple little statement which I suppose I am entitled to do which nobody need really object to except Silas since it uniquely refers to my bother Silas, I mean my brother Silas that is not my—

SILAS [drily] Not my vulgar Cockney half-brother that—

MRS. DAVENPORT Not my brother Silas that was, since my brother Silas that was apparently metamorphosed himself into an entirely different entity in the brother Silas that is; whilst I think a certain pungency and point will be injected into my little promulgation by a grateful acknowledgment to my daughter, Queenie, for her inspired discovery that Ewn Andzale is an anagram of New Zealand, and her equally penetrating and inspired discovery that I expected our deliverer to come from New Zealand. [waves arms and stares at SILAS] Therefore, hearken all ye people, raise your eyes to heaven and in the transformation you see before you in the person of my brother Silas is not my brother Silas that was—Behold Ewn Andzale has arrived!

[CISSIE, CAPTAIN DAVENPORT and POPHAM cheer widly]

POPHAM [gleefully] She's shrivelling—

DAVENPORT Shivering—

POPHAM She's shivering like a ghost and is as pale as an apsen leaf.

SILAS [quizzically] You'd take it better Queenie if your mother wasn't so patronising and hadn't assumed such a tantalising air of superiority.

QUEENIE [quietly] I daresay you're right uncle, but even more tantalising is the gloating of those three people opposite me, though they should know that even if I were capable of meeting mother on her own ground, which I am not, I would not dream of being so infilial as to make any riposte which might cause her any pain or humiliation, whilst, on the other hand, nobody's more glad

163

of mother's victory over me than I am myself, if it were only for the immense physical prophylactic benefits which I am certain will accrue to her therefrom. Here endeth the first lesson.

[*There is a constrained silence,* CISSIE *and* CAPT. DAVENPORT *and* POPHAM *looking before them and seeming nonplussed whilst* SILAS *takes cigarette from case. Suddenly* CISSIE *seems to get a brainwave and goes and puts on a gramophone record of the old French air,* '*Malborough s'en va t'en guerre*'. *As air is being played* MRS. DAVENPORT *seems to come to some inward resolution and with wan smile on face goes with somewhat uncertain steps to* QUEENIE]

MRS. DAVENPORT [*tremulously, placing hand on* QUEENIE'S *shoulder*] Queenie!

QUEENIE [*ditto*]: Mother! [*They embrace quietly, a slight sob is heard.*]

CURTAIN

First Production of the Plays

The Toothache. This play has not been produced.

The Country Dressmaker.

Presented by the National Theatre Society Limited at the Abbey Theatre Dublin, 3 October 1907

Julia Shea, a country dressmaker	Sara Allgood
Norry Shea, her mother	Bridget O'Dempsey
Matt Dillane, their next-door-neighbour	F. J. Fay
Min, his daughter	Maire O'Neill
Pats Connor, a returned American	J. M. Kerrigan
Edmund Normyle	J. A. O'Rourke
Michael Clohesy, a strong farmer	Arthur Sinclair
Maryanne, his wife	Maire O'Neill
Their Daughters:	
Babe	Eileen O'Doherty
Ellie	Cathleen Mullamphy
Jack, their son	T. J. Fox
Luke Quilter, the man from the Mountains	W. G. Fay

Produced by W. G. Fay

One Evening Gleam.

Presented by the Fortune Society at the Studio Theatre Club Dublin, 15 September 1952

Mrs. Cleary	Pat Saunders
Jim, her son	John Edwin
Mrs. Hannaigan	Pauline Browne
Phoebe Tollemache	Kitty O'Brien

Produced by Liam Miller
Decor by Nevill Johnson

'Twixt the Giltinans and the Carmodys

*Presented by the National Theatre Society Limited at the Abbey
Theatre Dublin, 8 March 1923*

Bileen Twomey	Arthur Shields
Shuwawn, his aunt	Eileen O'Kelly
Old Jane	May Craig
Michael Clancy	Michael J. Dolan
Simon Giltinan	F. J. McCormick
Mrs. Giltinan	Maureen Delany
Bridie Giltinan	Eileen Crowe
Madge Carmody	Gertrude Murphy
Mrs. Carmody	Christine Hayden
Jamesie Carmody	Peter Nolan

Produced by Lennox Robinson

The Coming of Ewn Andzale. This Play has not been produced.

The Simple Hanrahans. This Play has not been produced.

Boston Public Library

Copley Square

General Library

The Date Due Card in the pocket indicates the date on or before which this book should be returned to the Library. Please do not remove cards from this pocket.